D1626792

The Great Mosque of Isfahan

THE GREAT MOSQUE OF ISFAHAN

Oleg Grabar

I.B.TAURIS & Co Ltd
Publishers
London

Published by
I.B.Tauris & Co Ltd
110 Gloucester Avenue
London NW1 8JA

British Library Cataloguing in Publication Data
Grabar, Oleg
  The Great Mosque of Isfahan
  1. Islamic architecture, 1360–1570
  I. Title
  722'.52

ISBN 1-85043-185-X

Manufactured in the United States

For Anne-Louise

Contents

Illustrations

Introduction

The subject of this book and of the lectures that led to it is simple
enough: the celebrated Masjid-e Jomeh, or Friday Mosque, in Isfahan. It is difficult now to recapture my fascination as a graduate
student and as a beginning teacher with some of its parts, like the
court itself or the north dome; it was a fascination born of reading
about the building and looking over and over again at the same
photographs. Then there were several visits during a cold and rainy
spring of 1961, and I still remember the enchanted loneliness of
walking through its brick piers as I was trying to understand the
chronology of its supports and floors, the somber solidity of the
south dome and the total mystery of its massive supports, the off-
and-on jumping light that, like a magical beacon from above, led to
the north dome, the long walks in the midst of the domical bubbles
on its roof, and many more visual impressions partially recorded by
my companion of those days, a Leica M3 on a wobbly tripod. A
seminar on the mosque in the mid or late sixties at the University of
Michigan compelled me to put some order to my visual impressions,
to devise a tentative terminology for the building's constructional
technology, to survey the monuments of the area, and especially to
review such evidence as could be found in the common historical
and geographical sources of the Muslim Middle Ages. A study sum-

1

marizing my interpretation of the mosque was written for a grand book dedicated to the memory of Arthur Upham Pope, and I still do not quite know why the book never appeared. Retrospectively, this was a good thing for my study, for, in the meantime and quite unbeknownst to me, the Istituto Italiano per il Medio e Estremo Oriente, known to most scholars as ISMEO, took over the task of restoring, repairing, and surveying a crumbling building, some of whose parts began to be covered with scaffolding or closed off to visitors. Directed by Dr. Eugenio Galdieri, who had been part of the team that had so spectacularly restored the Ali Qapu and other Safavid palaces, the ISMEO mission did not only do its technical job of restoration remarkably well, but it also undertook important soundings to understand the past of the mosque and made many of its results and the conclusions derived from them available in a series of publications, three volumes of which have appeared so far. Accurate, even if partial, archaeological data, two or three additional trips to Isfahan, and a true information revolution that overwhelmed our knowledge of Islamic architecture in Iran during the seventies (and whose results are only now beginning to be seen) led to another seminar on the mosque, this time at Harvard University. And, finally, the invitation to deliver the Kevorkian lectures at New York University, on which this book is based, seemed like an appropriate occasion to express publicly and formally my views about a building that had been on my mind for more than a quarter of a century.

I begin in this autobiographical way for two reasons. One is that, together with two generations of students and scholars, I had become quite involved at different times of my own intellectual development with the Great Mosque of Isfahan, and it seemed appropriate to make available for further discussion and further research views that may have become more idiosyncratic than is justified. The other reason is that there always remained, after every visit or every seminar lecture about it, the sense of fascinated frustration that the building had still escaped me, that there was more to it than I had imagined or figured out. As I trust this book will show, there is a mystery, or at least an anomaly, about this monument, especially when it is viewed together with its presumed family of buildings, the large urban mosques of classical Islamic civilization.

The peculiarities of the mosque are sufficiently numerous and original that a way had to be devised to present the building so that

2

the problems it poses can be easily perceived. It is for this reason that I began with two separate descriptions of the building, corresponding to two ways of "learning" or "reading" a monument of architecture. One is broad and based on two-dimensional documents; the other is more concrete and centered on the experience and perception of an actual visitor in the building. These descriptions led, first of all, to a historical-chronological problem, which occupies the third chapter, and then to an interpretative one, which serves as a conclusion. Throughout I tried to intertwine the specifics of Isfahan's mosque with broader issues involved in the architectural analysis by today's viewer of the buildings of the past. The point is not an idle one, for I shall have more than one occasion to show how often interpretations of the mosque derived from preestablished views of what a mosque of a given time should be before the date of the mosque had been established.

The photographs have been chosen so as to provide as understandable a survey as possible, and nearly all the drawings have been adapted from the ones published in the three ISMEO volumes, with the kind permission of Dr. Galdieri. One practical adaptation had to be made. On each drawing the correct cardinal points are indicated, but, in order to simplify the text, the qiblah or direction of prayer is always south in the text and the other four sides of the mosque are defined accordingly. Similarly, transliterations have been simplified to the maximum allowed for comprehension, and Koranic references are according to the standard Egyptian version with translations adapted by me from several existing versions. Otherwise, the book is substantially the text of the lectures with a few additions to clarify some of the descriptions, with the removal of references that would only make sense in a lecture hall, and with a complement of notes with bibliographical references.

One of the curious byproducts of the preparation for the lectures and the book, and of the intervals between my concerns with the building, has been that satisfactory photographs are still not available. There must exist a reasonable median between the mass of accurate details, which trivialize a building, and the grandly impressive helicopter shot, which shows a building as seen only by angels. The relationship between photographer and historian has not yet been developed to the point that exists between architect and photographer; the photographer still does not know how to translate

3

into images the thoughts of the historical writer. The discourse of the historian is, in the final analysis, not a visual one, even if it is inspired by visual knowledge, while the eye of the modern critic, most of the time a Westerner fearful of non-Western art, has not transferred to the past its sensitivity to contemporary architecture. I have tried to go beyond the accepted ways of traditional monographs and to develop a descriptive vocabulary and especially an interpretative approach that may serve as a useful model for analyses of other buildings.

One last introductory remark. The purpose of this book and of the four lectures that are the basis for its text is to define and explain a specific building, as it stands today, however strange and complex its history may have been. What I did not do, because it would have required considerable expansion of text and image, is to locate the mosque of Isfahan within the art, ideology, and technology of its several times. Questions or issues like the origin and value of baked brick as a medium, the dome on muqarnas squinches, the techniques and styles of ornament, the origins of color in architecture, the four-iwan plan, the madrasah, and many others that have consistently and rightfully exercised scholars dealing with the mosque of Isfahan have been reserved for some other place and for others to handle. It was a conscious decision, as I wanted to concentrate on one object as an architectural phenomenon and not, as it is more frequently examined, the fulcrum of formal, functional, and ideological linear developments.

Five years ago Eugenio Galdieri asked me to write an introduction to his most recent book on the mosque and its archaeological exploration. His argument was that a historian of art and culture, which he claimed not to be, should introduce the work of the architect and archaeologist. But perhaps what the historian creates is a fiction of his imagination that satisfies his mind and his prejudices but does not explain a building. This is why I have asked Dr. Galdieri to contribute a postscript to this essay. The building, which he knows better than anyone else, has the right to respond to what is said about it and to be the last one to speak.

It is a pleasure to record my gratitude to the Hagop Kevorkian Center for Near Eastern Studies of New York University for having invited me to be the 1987 Kevorkian lecturer. It was particularly

4

gratifying to me that the invitation was extended by Dr. R. Bayly Winder, my teacher and friend of so very many years. Bayly has died since the lectures were given, and I, like many others, am the poorer for it. Dr. Doris S. Miller, assistant director of the center, smoothed a lot of practical details and I am grateful for that. Help in gathering data and in making drawings was given by Linda Lourie and Richard Brotherton. Photographs, when not my own, were provided by IS-MEO's archives, and, for this, as well as for a friendly relationship now extending over fifteen years, I must thank Dr. Eugenio Galdieri, who is much more of a historian of art than he claims to be. The Freer Gallery of Art in Washington, which keeps the priceless Herz-feld Archives, was kind enough to provide three unusually early records of the mosque. As usual, special thanks are due to graduate students at the University of Michigan and Harvard, whose reactions during the elaboration of this book were its first criticisms but whose enthusiasm was also inspiring. More specific gratitude is due to Isa-belle Frank, who translated Dr. Galdieri's text; Margaret Ševčenko, who, as usual, forced me to be clearer than I sometimes wished to be; Renata Holod and Sheila Blair, who made specific contributions to the content of the book; and Katherine McCollum, who cheerfully faced the keyboard of the word processor and had to read my handwriting.

I would like, lastly, to recall with some fondness the late Hagop Kevorkian, in whose honor the New York University center is named. His was an extraordinary personality issued from worlds now long gone. I first encountered him when I was a graduate student in 1951 or 1952. I had the privilege a few years later of seeing many objects in his collection, now largely scattered, but I mostly remember a forceful and dedicated personality, whose love for the artistic heri-tage of the Middle East was not always matched by his feelings for contemporary scholars. He often criticized the latter for not under-standing the former. I don't know whether he would have approved of the interpretations of this book, but he can rest assured that they come from a true fascination with the mosque of Isfahan.

CHAPTER 1

The Mosque and the City

The Masjid-e Jomeh, or Great Mosque, or Friday Mosque, of Isfahan (fig. 1) was an obligatory stop on every tourist's visit to Iran for several decades. It acquired a peculiar aura among Iranists in the West, one of whom, in a sentence that sounds embarrassingly condescending in our time of cultural self-consciousness, referred to it in a private conversation as "the Chartres of Iran." Another Western historian wrote about "the ponderous reality of [its] enclosed spaces" filled with "arches that have the sweetness of a desired answer . . . , the experience of the subtleties of inert mass."[1] The meaning of these words by a critic of great sensitivity to the world of images, possessor of what art historians call an "eye," still escapes me completely, but their eloquent passion is clear. I also recall seeing a documentary film made for and by Iranian television which transformed the mosque into handsome images of color and form zooming at each other across the screen. The images were accompanied by a rhapsodic text full of historical errors and by beautiful pseudo-vernacular contemporary music especially composed for the movie. I will say more about the nature of historical truth with respect to monuments of architecture, about the danger of beautiful photographs taken by ignorant photographers, and about the more or less useful modes of expressing esthetic judgments and feelings, but the initial point is that the extraordinarily high reputation enjoyed by the Great Mosque of Isfahan is a very recent phenomenon. In 1892 Lord Curzon, a man of high classical taste, and a highly prejudiced believer in the ultimate superiority of Western culture, considered it to be "deprived of genuine artistic value."[2] The numerous travelers of the seventeenth and eighteenth centuries hardly mention it at all. A rough plan was drawn by Coste and a few drawings were published by him or by other nineteenth-century architects and explorers, but most of their work is either inaccurate or incomplete and none of them devote to the Great Mosque the attention they have given to the Safavid masterpieces around the Meydan-e Shah, the Imperial Square, or to the city's gardens and bazaars.[3]

Interest in and concern for the Safavid monuments have obviously not stopped. They were the first ones to be repaired and restored when considerable funds were provided for the preservation of national treasures in the 1960s. They remained, until the Islamic Revolution of 1979, the monuments of Isfahan most frequently visited by tourists, in part because of their greater proximity to most hotels. But among some visitors, mostly scholars of various specialties, architects, and younger Iranians, an almost passionate fascination with the Masjid-e Jomeh grew from the early 1930s onward. This fascination is closely tied to the epistemology of the mosque, that is to say to the body of ideas, questions, prejudices, interpretations, and methods of approach which have been, legitimately or not, imposed upon it. The identification of some of these reasons as well as of their implications is more than a traditional academic exercise in bibliographical expertise, for it helps in defining the dialogue between a monument and its viewers which over nearly fifty years has shaped our knowledge of the mosque, just as it has shaped the approach to it which will be developed in the course of this book.[4]

The first set of reasons can be called sociovisual. Architects, planners, and eventually urbanists became fascinated by the extraordinary way in which a huge building (170 by 140 meters) appears to melt into the city surrounding it (figs. 1 and 2). Its edges seem inseparable from the living fabric of a constantly changing city, yet its presence is unmistakable. The validity rather than mere convenience of aerial photographs in discussing monuments of architecture may be and should be a matter for debate, but it is easy to see from an aerial photograph how such a conclusion is reached about an architectural setting, and all those who have perused a certain kind of architectural writing over the past thirty years can immediately translate what they see on the photograph—shopping streets along the building, houses or warehouses nearby, de-emphasized accesses, walls common to the mosque and to some other function, and so on—into the cultural terms of a traditional or vernacular world with an equilibrium between monumental and man-scaled or street-scaled forms. There is (or so it seems) an organic, living, relationship between all aspects of the built environment.[5] It is easy to imagine the next step, which may indeed have been taken unbeknownst to me, and to see the Isfahan building as a paradigm for a certain vision of a traditional Islamic city. It is a vision in which living, working, and worshiping God are intimately tied together and befit beautifully the Koranic prescription (62:9–10): "O ye who believe! When the call is proclaimed to prayer on Friday, Hasten earnestly to the remembrance of God and leave off business; this is the best for you if you but knew. And when prayer is finished, then may you disperse through the land."

A second group of reasons are esthetic and visual. Whether dilapidated as it appears in many old photographs or restored as it is today, the court of the mosque (figs. 3–6) has a breathtaking effect on its visitor, especially after the darkness of the covered areas which surround it; it is indeed like a new light bursting out of the tile-covered uprights and contrasting with the blackness of the voids. And then 476 cupolas in one building, almost all of them different from each other, create a festival of vaulting which does not fail to arouse all but the most jaded designers or historians. The cupolas can be seen from the outside as a sea of bubbles (fig. 7) from which occasionally emerges an exhilarating island of arches and segments of vaults (fig. 8). Or they can be followed inside the building, as one moves around with or without purpose and reaches the stunning composition of the north dome (fig. 9). Nearly everywhere, on wall surfaces or on vaulted ceilings fascinating, infinitely complex or strikingly simple designs (figs. 15, 17, 40, and others) catch the visitor's eye and offer a spectacle of formal exercises rarely found elsewhere with the variety and brio of Isfahan's Great Mosque. In fact, these motifs belong to many very different periods and fulfill

9

very different purposes, but such considerations can easily be explained away as expressions of a more or less timeless single Islamic or Irano-Islamic artistic tradition. Following an argument which can be used for religious architecture everywhere, the changes required by continuous use become incorporated into a building by timeless piety and are not to be judged or evaluated in chronological terms.

It is, however, precisely the differences in time which are at the root of the third set of reasons for the mosque's popularity. They are historical reasons. The very first publications and reports on the building made it clear that it had a long and complex chronology. These publications all provided schematic drawings of formal evolution in which different kinds of hatching were meant to be transformed in a viewer's mind into dynastic or other modifications to some earlier creation (fig. 10). The methodological implication of such drawings is dubious, but as a sort of *aide-mémoire* once you already know a building, they are certainly useful. The important historical point of Isfahan's Great Mosque was, however, much more specific than the fact of a long history. Its two largest and most impressive cupolas (figs. 20 and 41) with totally new features in Iranian Islamic architecture are dated to the second half of the eleventh century. Simplifying matters a little bit at this stage, Isfahan's examples form in fact the earliest dated evidence for a technological and esthetic revolution in Iranian architecture. Furthermore the period is that of the Seljuq "saviors" of the mainstream Sunni caliphate in Baghdad against all heresies; of Nizām al-Mulk's Irano-Turano Islamic ideological synthesis (his name is in fact on one of the domes), of the great theologian and philosopher al-Ghazali, whose name symbolizes the new religious and philosophical equilibrium between revelation, reason, law, and experience, and of the poet and mathematician Omar Khayyam who lived in Isfahan. It is, then, easy to understand how the building was seen as the paradigm of a new epoch in medieval Islamic civilization. The Masjid-e Jomeh became in books and articles the "Seljuq" mosque of Isfahan, and a spontaneous but nonetheless reprehensible academic and para-academic publicity transformed certain parts of the mosque into demonstrations of national genius and of a revolutionary technology which was going to influence, in Western architecture, the passage from Romanesque to Gothic.[6]

Finally, there are archaeological reasons to become interested in

10

the mosque of Isfahan. By the term "archaeological" I do not mean only the application to it of a certain technique of acquiring information. I also mean the availability of nearly complete information about many parts of the building. Thanks to Lutfallah Hunarfar's painstaking gathering of all inscriptions visible around 1960,[7] an essential body of documents for traditional Islamic architecture is available. The inscriptions are published more or less as they appear to someone walking through the building rather than in chronological order. They are shown as they should be, as the verbal message of the mosque, not as a sequence of epigraphic documents. Newly discovered inscriptions can easily be added.[8]

Furthermore, surveys, soundings, and excavations were carried out by the first-rate Italian team from ISMEO directed by Eugenio Galdieri for the architectural and restoration work and by Umberto Scerrato for excavations per se. A great deal of new information has come out of this work, new plans and drawings of unusual accuracy were made, a few sections of the building were excavated, and a number of reconstructions were proposed. The structure of the mosque's vaults, the chronology of its supports, and the original shapes of the south and north dome areas are by now as well documented as they ever shall be. Three volumes of the Italian excavations have been published and others are still to come.[9] Such problems as remain (and there are quite a few) must be resolved through means other than information in the building itself. The archaeological record of Isfahan's mosque is, of course, not complete. The whole building could be excavated. Masonry surveys and chemical analyses of plaster or of bricks could be extended systematically to the whole building. But, while more could indeed be done, a lot has been done in a systematic enough way to generate the validity of the evidence, that is to say the likely percentage it represents of all eventually available archaeological data.[10] Once new problems and new questions emerge, a possible strategy for further soundings or excavations could be developed. In the meantime, the building remains available for students, visitors, and the faithful.

Finally, the major literary sources, at least for the centuries which preceded the Mongol conquest, are fairly well accessible. Historical sources have been culled by Ann Lambton for a survey of the city's history in the *Encyclopaedia of Islam*. Two eleventh-century city histories of a genre well-known in Islamic historiography—Abu Nu'aym's

Dhikr Akhbar Isfahan and al-Mafarrukhi's *Kitab Mahasin Isfahan*—are readily available, and Paul Schwarz's survey of medieval Iran contains most of the additional known historical and geographical information.[11] Once again, with all caution because surprises can always occur, the sources for the first six centuries of Isfahan's history are as available as they are ever likely to be.

Archaeological, historical, and esthetic reasons have led to yet one more peculiarity of the epistemology of the Great Mosque. There are differing views about it, and a modicum of debate and discussion that are sufficiently rare in the study of Islamic art as to merit comment. Specialists of Iranian Islamic architecture like Godard, Schroeder, Pope, and Galdieri have written about the mosque of Isfahan and have sharply disagreed about it.[12] In addition, Galdieri, Sauvaget, Ettinghausen, and I came to the mosque from other interests and other concerns, as though each one of us was made to feel that something of unusual importance was found there.[13] Only one other monument of Islamic architecture, the Haram al-Sharif in Jerusalem, and more specifically its two jewels, the Dome of the Rock and the Aqsa Mosque, can boast the same variety and completeness of data and the same diversity of scholarly attention. The parallel between the two monuments is not entirely fortuitous, as I shall argue further on. A handful of other monuments of Islamic architecture, the mosque of Damascus, a few Cairene buildings, the Alhambra, the Süleymaniye, the Tāj Mahal, are provided with the same range of documents and a comparable degree (in a few cases even more) of gushing rhetoric, but they lack that scholarly meditation of nearly half a century which has endowed the Great Mosque of Isfahan and the Dome of the Rock with an intellectual uniqueness, even if its implications have not penetrated into the more general surveys of Islamic architecture.

How does one deal with an apparently unique building? One approach is to deconstruct it and to trivialize it into a sum of amorphous elements, like bricks or geometric ornament, or of forms, like iwans or muqarnas domes. Elements or forms are then related to sets of parallels and comparisons elsewhere which establish the chronology and value of the building through the peculiar composition and mass of forms and elements found in it. Or one argues that the apparent uniqueness is in fact a real one, whose characteristics and forms of expression must indeed be identified within the redundant

12

trivia of a period or area style, but also, and perhaps primarily, be explained within itself, as a closed syntagm of elements from many sources.

These queries can be put more specifically. We can argue a priori that a monument of architecture of the size and apparent coherence of the Masjid-e Jomeh cannot be the result of haphazard constructions glued together, but requires the existence at some time of a major architectural creation, against or around which all further developments took place. The historian's objective is to identify that moment and to explain how it came to create whatever it did. In other words, the original synchronic understanding of the monument comes first, and the normal task of the historian of architecture is so often to divest an existing monument of all its later accretions and to present it in its pristine purity. This search for an *Ur*-state may indeed turn out to be important in dealing with our Great Mosque, but it is so evident that it underwent many changes and that many ensembles were attached to it or forced on it, that it is clearly a monument with a diachronic dimension of some significance. To have had a history is part of its character and it is a fairly rare one, as a constant diachronic evolution is not characteristic of mosques (with a few exceptions to be brought out in the last chapter), but of holy places—Mekkah, Madinah, Jerusalem, Meshhed—and of nearly all imperial or royal palaces from Rome to Versailles. Thus, in Isfahan, the very fact of diachronic significance leads to questions about the building's meaning through the unusual company it seems to keep.

Let us assume or suppose, however, that both the synchrony of the moment of creation and the diachronic significance of change through the centuries can be described and explained satisfactorily. What we would have achieved is an illustrated text for the use of the scholarly academic profession. For the appreciation of history, whether evolutionary or of a moment, is an acquired taste which has its own demands and prerequisites like a need or a desire to feel and understand a past long gone. Yet a work of architecture, and especially one which is still in use apparently with its original functions, has a contemporary meaning. Ours are not the concerns and needs of the past, and whether one seeks to emphasize older esthetic values or adapt them to new ones, whether one repairs or restores, whether one emphasizes the purity of brick surfaces of the relationship of the mosque to the city, in all cases the choices and judgments we make reflect a variety of contemporary ideologies which use the past but do not necessarily know or understand it.

Are there answers in the Masjid-e Jomeh of Isfahan to contemporary queries of planners, architects, or sociologists? Let me give but one example. I was struck during my first visit to Isfahan nearly thirty years ago by the paucity of worshipers in the Masjid-e Jomeh, as compared with the Darb-e Imam or the Masjid-e Ali, later and much redone sanctuaries of the city. I registered this fact without seeking to interpret it, and it was not until much later that I realized the existence of an internal Isfahani rhythm in the use of mosques. I was not then programmed to pursue this kind of question, but its importance for the Masjid-e Jomeh of Isfahan may well have opened up yet another approach to the study of the building and perhaps of many mosques elsewhere.

This rather lengthy introduction to a series of lectures includes two themes which explain how I have organized the lectures themselves and, therefore, the order of the book. The first theme is that of the physical, visual, historical, esthetic, and scholarly complexity of a building which may well be a mosque but is not like most other mosques one knows. The second theme is that the understanding of an ancient building is inseparable from the web of questions, prejudices, and ideological or sensual predispositions brought to it. A unique object is in large part made unique by the one who looks at it, and it is a sort of dialogue with the mosque that I would like to initiate.

First, however, we must "learn" the mosque, initially through plans and aerial photographs, then in a more visually and experientially coherent way through eyes and feet. Only then will it become possible to propose a chronology of the mosque and finally an explanation of its meaning. In keeping with the sequence of the lectures, the balance of this chapter and the following one propose two visual readings of the mosque, while the last two chapters will interpret it historically and then semantically.

The aerial photograph is an unreal way of perceiving a building (figs. 1 and 2). No one except birds sees it from the air, and no architect or artisan composes a structure from the point of view of the proverbial flying crow. The drawn plan (fig. 11) is equally unreal

14

in that it is a translation into conventional lines and dots of an actual or imaginary building. Although not as new as the aerial photograph, it is a relatively recent mode for seeing and even more recent for composing a building.[14] In other words, the two modes of information used to introduce the mosque of Isfahan are fairly new, or even quite contemporary modes which played no part in the creation of our "object." They serve primarily to help us, contemporary observers sitting outside the object, to comprehend it, because they transform a three-dimensional object into a two-dimensional document and therefore make architecture immediately available, as the techniques and methods of visual analysis have been far better developed for painting and drawings than for architecture. The two images, a plan and an aerial photograph, are the only introductions to a building which are comprehensible away from the space the building occupies and which therefore provide the avenue for the third of the approaches to the mosque, its value in contemporary culture. Seen in this fashion, the mosque merges with the surrounding city. The absence of clear edges is apparent both on the photograph and on the plan.

It is, furthermore, reasonable to use the negative "absence" rather than to find a more positive way of describing and explaining this merging. An example of the latter would be something like the symbiosis of the daily and of the sacred in a single mass, an explanation fitting with a traditionalist understanding of the Muslim past. Such a positive reading of the mosque's relationship to the city seems to me, at least at this stage of investigation, dubious because the lack of clarity of its edges differentiates Isfahan's mosque from the hundreds of known city mosques. In the seventh and eighth centuries new mosques of Kufa or Damascus, in the twelfth-century ones from Ardistan or Zavareh, which are supposed to be contemporary with Isfahan, and in the grand imperial mosques in Ottoman, Mughal, or Safavid architecture, the physical separation of the mosque from the city which contains it was visibly expressed through walls and, at times but according to less clearly established rhythms, through open spaces, in early times with the curious name of *ziyadah*, "addition."

Another consistent connection between a mosque and its surrounding spaces is the entrance, either multiple ones as in many early city mosques or limited in number but architecturally emphasized through a facade, as became common in later times. Facades were beginning to appear in the tenth century, and a striking example remains in Isfahan itself of the elaborate gate with ornamented facade to what has been identified as the Jorjir mosque (figs. 45–46).[15] The Masjid-e Jomeh does have multiple entries. Some of them are even provided with external facades, but none of them is clearly visible from the aerial photograph or even in the plan. In other words, the building, as we see it in these documents, lacks, at least in its contemporary shape, the two most common ways of defining its own space in relationship to its surroundings. It has no clear wall around it and no strongly emphasized access.

The organizing principle and the facade of the Isfahan mosque are not, in fact, on the outer periphery of the building but inside it, more or less in its center. There we find the mosque's one strongly anchored fixture, a central court, measuring 65 by 55 meters, with the rather unexciting proportions of 1:1.2; the court is provided with two rectangular platforms and with a fountain (figs. 3–6). Each side of the court is composed in a similar manner. There is a high iwan—consisting of a tall two-dimensional screen wall and of a vaulted hall behind—in the center. On either side of the iwan and, with only occasional minor modifications, two tiers of openings in a wall or a sequence of passages separated by piers seem rhythmically to repeat the shape of the iwan. There are several possible ways of interpreting these forms, but the essential point at this stage is that, in a striking esthetic procedure which is that of the Parthenon inside out, the compositional anchor, the starting point of the whole building, is its inner facade on the court. The center of the building, a court, is also the space from which the building begins; it then spreads out into the surrounding urban space.

When and how these particular forms were created is not apparent from the evidence, but differences between iwans are visible. The east and west ones are 12 meters square, the south one is 14 meters square, but the northern one is quite different, 22 by 9.4 meters. The proportions of the last, the square root of 3:4, are created by two adjacent equilateral triangles.[16] The iwans are covered with vaults— a barrel vault on the north iwan (fig. 3), and muqarnas vaults of different kinds on the other three (figs. 4–6). All the vaults are hidden by a high screen on the court, and the southern one is flanked by two towers which look suspiciously like what are usually called minarets, but prayer is called from a small pavilion, the *goldas-*

16

teh, located on the western screen (fig. 6). The iwans are also differ-ent from each other in plan. The western one is almost entirely closed except toward the courtyard; the eastern one contains a small passageway in the back; the southern one is connected with a huge doomed room on its own south side in front of an elaborate mihrab, and the northern one is unusual for its openness toward east and west and for its massive blocks of masonry to the north.

These iwans serve as axes for the organization of the space be-tween them. It is easy enough to identify on both of our documents a rectangle made out of the prolongation of the back wall (that is, the wall away from the court facade) of the iwans and including the south dome (figs. 42–44, 47–49). Within this rectangle the areas between iwans are divided into square bays, roughly 4 by 4 meters, which are covered with domes, those wonderful little bubbles of brick and plaster that appear on the roof (fig. 7).

But then something happens to what had been until now a reason-ably logical progression from a court to a facade with four strong axes perpendicular to the sides of the court, and eventually to a rectangle which would have been the outer edge of the mosque. The anomaly to this rational order is that the outer rectangle is a fiction everywhere but on the south side. In reality the structure of small square bays is extended towards the southeast and towards the north, where it eventually encases the celebrated northern dome with its stunning inner composition (fig. 9). Furthermore on the southeast-ern and western sides, there are three independent buildings with, at least in the case of the southeastern one, an interior composition independent of the whole mosque. All these independent units ap-pear to be glued to our arbitrary rectangle and can only be reached through it. Finally, in the northwestern quadrant, are the latrines, a large ablution area, and a mortuary, all normal and expected services for a mosque which are occasionally eccentric to the building's main scheme, as they are in Isfahan.

Additions and extensions are obvious enough, but the plan and to a lesser degree the aerial photographs also indicate exclusions. To the north and south of the western iwan, sections of the original building were walled off into separate little entities whose ceilings are higher than the adjoining one.

This rapid introduction to the masjid through two documents which provide a single image for the whole building leads to four conclusion-questions or conclusion-hypotheses, statements which, on the evidence adduced so far, *seem* to be true, but which pose problems or leave the observer uneasy with their implications.

Seen from afar, the mosque looms like an inkblot or a set of bubbles in a boiling cauldron. It is an inkblot on a plan in its apparent relationship to the city, while from the air its rows of cupolas erupting from a massive building suggest that something interesting, important, or exciting takes place inside the building. But these two characteristics are only obvious to or intended for outsiders, distant in space and time from the mosque, for they are only visible to those who are not in Isfahan. They are true but they are not part of a person's actual and normal experience of the monument. Yet these observations lead us to broad socio-architectural questions: Is the mosque invading the city? Or is the city absorbing the mosque? To whom does the mosque belong? Who repairs it and constantly covers it with the latest fashion—colored tiles, brick ornament, simple plaster? There is now, and probably there always has been, a very special relationship between the city and the building, as some urban order was ultimately responsible for its maintenance. What is interesting is that the question and nature of this symbiosis between city and mosque are so forcefully posed by the two-dimensional perception of the building.

The space of the mosque is composed from its central facade on the court outward and could be schematized in terms of four axes of order through the middle of each iwan and of a series of extensions and/or additions. There were even instances of exclusions. A priori these modifications could be chronological, reflecting changes in taste or technology, functional responses to some new need or activity, or both. New purposes could lead to additions or to abandonments of parts of buildings, as happened for instance both in Cordova and in the Aqsa mosque in Jerusalem, but these were mosques composed in the additive hypostyle mode which easily allows for changes. Although also in a hypostyle mode, a more comparable parallel is that of the Azhar mosque in Cairo, where a radical change of purpose led to masses of additions, but the hypostyle center was left relatively untouched. The central court-and-iwan mode of composition typical of Iran made such changes esthetically and visually more complicated than the hypostyle to achieve successfully. The

18

more important question, however, is whether these changes are functional ones or merely normal modifications brought to buildings by continuous use. Thus, a preliminary and external survey of the evidence demands answers of time and of purpose, of chronology, and of functions.

A third series of observations dealt with what may be called artistic technology, that is to say, the consistency and competence of the constructional and compositional techniques used. It is obvious enough that we are dealing with a baked-brick architecture which had developed a set of devices—squinches, muqarnas, zones of transition, domes, ornamental uses, colored tiles, or glazed bricks—which are not systematically alike throughout the building but which belong to the same basic idiom. This idiom was not only a vocabulary, a list of terms; it was also a manner of ordering space through the axial iwans separating any shape into four quadrants. This order in fact divided space into equal units separated from each other by massive walls on every side except the northern one. It was possible to maintain the canonically and liturgically required direction toward Mekkah through a dominating dome, but the internal unity of space characteristic of early Islamic mosques was broken. Why? Was it simply a question of not having the technological competence to solve a problem of larger space by using a compositional system based on iwans for congregational function? The quality of the construction makes it highly unlikely that the sponsors and builders or decorators of the building did not have access, whenever this intervention took place, to the most sophisticated technology available. The scheme of the mosque was a deliberate choice, and it is therefore legitimate to ask what led to it. Furthermore, why is there a second large dome on the same axis as the first one, but at the opposite end of the present mosque?

Nearly all these questions and queries lead to a far more fundamental issue. Why is it that a mosque still in use for what was presumably its original function—and we all know what a mosque is —constantly leads its viewer, even at a distance, toward the building's history? For this constant appeal to sequences of time is hardly typical of the architecture of the mosque, whose actual activities are relatively constant. Changes of taste or details of organization, like the replacement of muezzins by tapes, have not affected a basic continuity of function. A historicity of function and an abundance of diachronic reminders of different tastes are, on the other hand, typical of many shrines, of the Azhar in Cairo, and of urban palaces. Is the Masjid-e Jomeh more than a mosque? The question is intriguing enough that we may as well visit the mosque in the normal way, with our feet and eyes.

CHAPTER 2

A Tour of the
Mosque

We have seen how a plan and two aerial photographs transformed the Masjid-e Jomeh of Isfahan into a two-dimensional object, but allowed us to perceive it completely and at a single glance. The mosque appeared to have been generated from a fixed interior facade on court—what was earlier called the esthetics of the Parthenon inside out—and to have spread horizontally like an inkblot into the surrounding city and vertically like a cauldron boiling with domical bubbles. It was also clear that it is a building with a history, as additions and even subtractions modified a hypothetically simple and coherent original scheme.

There is, however, another way of experiencing a building, on one's feet and using one's eyes. This is what this chapter will try to do. Such a presentation should, in principle, incorporate every bit of archaeological and epigraphic information that still exists and has been retrieved, so that the perception of the building and feeling for it can be as total as possible. In reality, of course, totality of perception is impossible to achieve and also probably unnecessary, but the very idea that totality of perception may not be necessary leads to one of the cores of art historical procedure. The perception I (or anyone else) have of what I see is not really a neutral and, so to speak, clinical act. It is one which is already loaded either with methodological or historical prejudices. For instance, much of my own thinking about the mosque assumes the existence of an idea about a completed building from a specific type or style of which this building is a variant. Others, like Sauvaget or Godard, were so concerned with historical issues such as the importance of madrasahs in the eleventh and twelfth centuries that they tended to see traces of this ideologically charged educational institution in whatever was built during those centuries.[1] All too easily one's reading of a building becomes a search for clues to advance already developed theories and interpretations under the guise of scientific completeness. I cannot claim to have avoided preinterpreting the evidence of the mosque, and especially I cannot say that I saw everything that was visible. What follows must, therefore, be evaluated less in terms of true or false observations than in terms of verisimilitude and of usefulness: Is it likely that this or that statement about the mosque is true? Does it help in understanding the mosque?

This is the level of description and presentation of architecture which is most difficult to achieve successfully, because the evidence can almost never really be tested, especially not through two-dimensional photography. Looking at a work of architecture is, in many ways, like watching a televised football game; it can only be understood, even by professionals, if several cameras are constantly focused on what is going on, and instant replays are always available from whatever point of view may suddenly become necessary.

On a more concrete level, even though a survey of the vaults was carried out by ISMEO,[2] the visual evidence for the mosque is not complete. Furthermore, since it is a living building, in a living city, it even now changes constantly; thus a difference of twenty years makes the same areas look quite different, to the great disgust of slide librarians whose Rembrandts are not so unreliable. I shall therefore be talking about a building as it existed around 1970 (the date of most of the photographs that appear in these pages), for which my own primary experience is almost ten years earlier, and whose major studies are a generation earlier than that, but I will add archaeologically retrieved information and architectural reconstructions (essentially Galdieri's work) which are from the 1980s. Whether these differences in dates are in this particular instance significant or not

22

is perhaps not overly important, except, as I shall show in the last chapter, for interpretations, but the point is a methodologically important one in any study of an architectural monument.[3] And, in the instance of our mosque, Galdieri's initial perception of the building and his decisions on where to excavate or what to investigate were based on Godard's reconstructions, themselves affected by his own special theory of the formation of Iranian mosques. And now Galdieri's new directions will influence all students of the building.

The description which follows is thus incomplete, because of the unevenness of the documentation available for it and because I have concentrated on two issues and left out a third. The ones which seemed to me dictated by my own initial assessment of the mosque's uniqueness are its history and its meaning. Formal, technical, and stylistic questions play a lesser part in the visit I am proposing. They could be the subject of another trip.

ACCESSES

There are three kinds of accesses to the mosque of Isfahan as there are to nearly any building in an urban context. The first one is remote access. Where does one become aware of the mosque and how is one led to it? The appearance of a building from afar is an aspect of urban analysis in the Islamic world[4] which has been little studied. Because it has not been raised at all for Isfahan and because my own awareness of the issue is a relatively recent one, the available evidence is very partial, but two sets of observations seem reasonable enough.

The first one is that, since the mosque does not possess elements of unusual height, only the two towers of its south iwan and the large south and north domes serve as signs for awareness from afar. They can only be seen from within fairly large open areas like caravanserais or fancy houses. Furthermore, the higher features of the masjid are not differentiated enough from their surroundings (as opposed, for instance, to the thin towers of the Seljuq period)[5] to be easily identifiable from afar as significant landmarks. But these observations must be handled with care. They certainly apply to the contemporary building and are probably valid from the sixteenth century on. Matters may well have been quite different earlier.

The second remote access is the celebrated covered path which leads away from the Safavid ensemble, meanders through the bazaar, and ends by the Masjid-e Jomeh (fig. 12). Even today, in spite of momentous urban changes, the natural pedestrian flow in the streets of Isfahan always leads to the mosque whose south dome occasionally appears through an opening in the fabric of the city. This pedestrian access was provided through the rhythms of life, not through a formal processional way. In this it fits in with a dominant Muslim tradition which, until the Safavids and the Mughals, avoided a clearly delineated system of formal or visual access to major monuments and replaced them with subtler and less immediately perceptible signaling, as in the case of Cairene gates and minarets.[6] The peculiarities of Isfahan's signs now and in the past have not been worked out or discussed.

A nearer access to the building lies on its immediate edges, essentially its outer border, delineated walls (fig. 13) or walls shared with the nearest buildings. As was apparent on aerial photographs and plans, there is no way of walking around the building; its walls are often undetectable and certainly do not form the continuous curtain typical of the large urban mosques of Islam. Furthermore, and perhaps more significantly, there is no indication of any consistent activity near or around the mosque, except in the very general way that there are shops. Once again, the evidence of the second half of the twentieth century need not be valid for the past, but, at this stage, it is appropriate to consider whatever information happens to be available and to conclude that the physical independence of the mosque was not made visible through the appearance of the fabric of the building nor through some discrete events leading to it. It is almost as though the activities of the city are leaning against the mosque which would have been an accidental and unexpected space within the urban fabric. A quality which, from an urbanist's point of view mentioned in the previous chapter, could be praised as a wonderful example of symbiosis between praying and living, between city and monument, can be understood as a set of opposite, although not necessarily, antagonistic energies: the closed and restricted mosque in the midst of noisy life.

The third way of granting access to the mosque is through entries, doors, or gateways. It should be easy to find out how many entrances are known to exist or to have existed, but it is in fact quite difficult to do so, even in today's building. Although the justification for all of

24

these would take a whole seminar, nine gates, whether all visible today or not, can be proposed for the present wall enclosing the mosque. Of these nine gates, one on the east side is presumed to have existed before modern constructions, two on the south side are secondary service entrances, and one or two (the evidence is unclear, around plan areas 323–27[7] and certainly 391 dated 1301/1883–84) near the ablution area and the mortuary and fulfill secondary purposes for the building. This leaves us with four gates of some substance:

1. In the southeastern area (84), the gate which is the present entrance to the mosque was repaired in 1218/1803–4 during a program of restorations *(ta'amīr)*. The inscription commemorating this work refers to the gate as the "gate of the old Masjid-e Jomeh" and mentions also the building of a fountain and of a suq endowed for the mosque.[8] The exact date of the original gate is unknown, but an undated inscription just inside the mosque (area 85) near a passageway leading to the madrasah in the northeastern corner of the ensemble gives the name of the Muzaffarid sultan Mahmud who ruled in Isfahan between 1358 and 1374. Nearly all writers, from Godard to Galdieri, have assumed that this area became a gate in the second half of the fourteenth century, recognizing the possibility of an earlier access, now lost.

2. In the southwestern quadrant (282), a gate dated 999/1590–91, from the time of Shah Abbas, is still in use today and, together with the previous gate which is on the same level, permits the use of the mosque as a passage from one quarter of the city to another. This use of mosques is not unusual; as for instance in Damascus, where the mosque is so centrally located within the urban fabric and so large that it hinders natural urban communications.

3. On the north side (area 475) is a large monumental gate, unused today (fig. 14). Its inscription has largely disappeared, but from the end of it that remains it can be surmised that it contained verses 1–27 of surah 76, *al-Dahr*. This holy fragment comprises one of the many eschatological passages of the Koran, with a particularly luxurious description of eternal life. It ends with the following statement:

And celebrate [or recall, *udhkur*] the name of the Lord morning and evening and part of the night, prostrate thyself to Him *(usjud lahu)*, and glorify Him a long night through *(laylan tawīlan)*. As for these [i.e., non-pious people], they love the fleeting life and put away behind them a Day that will be at hand [i.e., the Day of Reckoning].

The gate is dated 1366, and its message of mystical vigils rather than of daily prayers is clearly legible at eye level on the left of the doorway as one enters the mosque.[9] It should be added that this gate is not aligned to any axis derived from the mosque, but is in all likelihood related to something in the surrounding city.

4. In the northeastern quadrant, in area 433, is found another disused formal gateway with brick instead of colored-tile decoration (fig. 15). Enough of its inscription is left to ascertain that it included Koran 2:114:

And who is more unjust than he who forbids that in places for the worship of God (masājid) God's name should be celebrated, whose zeal is in fact to ruin them? It was not fitting that such [people] should themselves enter these [places of worship] except in fear. For them there is nothing but disgrace in this world and in the world to become an exceeding torment.

This passage is often quoted in scholarly discussions about the mosque and its origins, but it is relatively rarely found on monuments. Clearly it refers to some particularly revolting form of desecration that had befallen the mosque.[10] The inscription adds, however, that this building (ʿimārah) was restored after a fire in 515/1121–22.[11] Significantly, the word used is the most general one that exists in Arabic to indicate a building.

Two major conclusions and one minor one can be deduced from the gates. One is that, at some early time, the main access to the mosque was from the north, but that under Shah Abbas the present east and west areas of primary entry were stabilized and the others possibly closed. For reasons yet to be investigated, a shift occurred in the relationship of the mosque to the city. But none of the gates, early or late, are in a location whose logic would be dictated by the mosque; they all reflect some rhythm of life belonging to the city. This is not in itself unusual, as such gates did broadcast the mosque to the city, but there is something unusual in the fact that the two earliest remaining gates are also set obliquely to the main axes of the mosque, as though the city and its mosque were at odd angles with each other.

The second conclusion is that each of these early gates contains a

26

specific message in the Koranic language appropriate for such messages. There is a reference to a destruction by fire through human violence before 1121–22 and an invitation to practice a certain form of piety around 1366. One is a political message, the other a cultural and religious one. Later gates lack this intensity of fervor and, when inscribed, refer only to repairs. Is it intensity of life or faith which, at some point, waned around the mosque? Or were gates no longer the place for pious messages?

The more minor conclusion is minor only because there is not much that one can do about it. It is likely that not all of these accesses to the mosque over the centuries have been preserved and therefore that the information gathered from the ones that do remain must therefore be handled with caution. But this is a problem solely for a historical reconstruction of the mosque; for an understanding of what the building is now, the point is irrelevant, because the gates which have been preserved already indicate the complexity of the relationship between mosque and city. Additional information would only confirm a reasonable conclusion.

THE COURT

Aerial photographs and the plan have identified the appropriate visual approach to the mosque as moving directly into the 65 by 55 meter court, for the monument's facade, and therefore its logical beginning, is there. What we see (figs. 3–6) is a screen of two-dimensional and, for the most part, very simple and often restored [12] color patterns of bricks or ceramics applied on a simple architectural design of vertical units of two superposed arches symetrically arranged around the deep recesses of the four iwans. The profile of nearly all openings is the same type of four-centered arch. Variants occur on the east side (fig. 4), where the screens on either side of the iwan are higher and on the northwest side (fig. 6), where there is a heavily decorated gateway in area 479 (fig. 16) with an inscription referring to the building of a "large edifice as a winter mosque" in 1447. It is the only instance of dated Timurid work in the building. [13] What it actually alludes to is a problem to be discussed in the following chapter.

On an archaeologically minute level it should be noted that nearly all the lower openings are passageways into dark areas, while the upper ones appear for the most part closed off by many different materials and methods. Many periods and especially many ranges of effort are clearly involved in the making of these barely accessible living and storage areas. Most are recent and of poor quality. From older photographs and other detailed observations, especially in the northeastern corner, it is clear that originally all these openings were alike and of a single story, as in the early twelfth-century mosque in Zavareh not too far away from Isfahan. What we see, therefore, are two kinds of modifications of the inner facade of the mosque. There are functional modifications which created a second story within much of the mosque and which, at some point, isolated the northern half of the western face into a separate building by providing it with a fancy gate. And there are formal, perhaps esthetic, modifications which gave different types of colored ornamentation to the facade, types which were probably constantly repaired and restored, so that at no time, except that of the hypothetic original mosque, was the elevation of the court completed and available according to a single esthetic and visual canon.

Soundings brought one additional element to the understanding of this facade on the court. Its emplacement corresponds exactly to the edges of the court of the second version of an earlier, hypostyle, mosque (fig. 18). That mosque is not dated directly, but a number of stylistic details as well as textual information to which I shall return in the following chapter make it certain that it was from the tenth century and belonged to the Buyid period. Unfortunately these were only soundings and not excavations, and therefore they did not bring to light any significant information (or, at least, none has been published) about the chronology of the construction of the now existing facade, about how presumably it replaced an earlier building.

In any event, the inner core of the present mosque was drawn out for a building which no longer exists; it was modified over time in all sorts of ways, and yet possesses a unity of formal and decorative character constantly renewed by colorful patterns and materials. It is also a facade with a contrast between highly lit and almost flattened fulls and dark voids in the areas between iwans, suggesting the possible use of the covered areas for some particular function, some precise activity. The facade is thus, on the one hand, an end in itself,

28

a nearly two-dimensional screen of designs applied on a building. But, on the other, it is a passageway with multiple ways of entering spaces otherwise unidentified and unexplained.

The iwans do not appear in the same fashion. Three of them have their back walls visible from the court: walls on the east and west, heavy walls with a wide opening toward a dark area to the south. The northern iwan seems, by contrast, open and accessible, a passageway rather than an ending.

These contrasts between sides, between fulls and voids, or between volumes and surfaces were not static. As the light of the sun moved, so did the values given to one segment of the facade over the others. In an architecture which so developed color surfaces, effectiveness and intensity depended a great deal on the operation of light. And this light altered, perhaps even contradicted, the rigid symmetry and axiality of the court's plan.

A curious point involving movement and the perception of the building in time is that from the center of the court none of the domes are really visible, neither the numerous small ones, nor the two large ones. The south or qiblah dome, however, becomes visible as one moves away from the center of the court toward the north, i.e., away from the qiblah itself, and then turns around to face the south iwan. It is as though the message of the dome was meant to be most effective as one came into the court from the north; it then disappeared from view, but presumably remained in memory as the eventual culmination of a visit to the mosque. This process of learning suggests an axis of perception and possibly composition for the mosque different from the one based on the central court. There would have been a north-south axis of movement in addition to the enclosed and circumambulatory axis of the court.

These observations can be put in yet another way. The facade on court consists of a sort of skin or tent flaps stretched on a series of fixed supports of masonry and creating deep recesses whose spaces are extensions of the court. These extensions are esthetically essential, for they further heighten the paradox of the court. On the one hand, its facade excludes it from the building, as it is on the "outside," the place *whence* the building is to be seen. On the other hand, its penetration of the built area through the means of iwans makes it an integral part of the whole ensemble.

29

The most important iwan, both visually and functionally, is the south one. It is followed by and seems intimately connected with a large domed room which has a tall mihrab indicating the direction of prayer. It is also the only iwan to have been framed by two thin vertical towers. Its present, vernacular, name is *sofe-e sāheb,* "the high [in a qualitative rather than descriptive sense] space of the Master." It contains an inscription dated 1475–76, the time of Uzun Hassan, the great ruler of the Aq Qoyunlu dynasty, mentioning the sorry shape of this magnificent mosque *(al-jāmi͑ al-munī͑)* and the restoration of the ceiling of the iwan. But the majority of its very numerous inscriptions are from the time of Shah Tahmasp (1531–32) and especially Shah Abbas II (1642–67).[14]

Pending a detailed study of these inscriptions, which are on the whole more important for social and cultural history than for architectural archaeology, two preliminary observations are pertinent to our purpose of understanding a building. One, a technical one, is the constant use in the inscriptions of two words, *ta͑mīr,* to restore or repair, and *taz'īn,* to embellish. Beyond its obviousness in identifying the two most consistent construction activities going on in any building, this observation makes the further point that neither this building nor in fact any old building is really in its original shape. The problem is only to assess the distance between an original monument and its present form. Or else we may indeed wonder whether, since the whole point of a public building like a mosque is to be used through time, it should not always be evaluated for its capacity for change rather than for its original qualities. The question is, in other words, whether, in contradiction to painting, where the historian always seeks to evaluate the initial impact of a work of art, architecture should not be judged in terms of its adaptability through time as well as in terms of its shape at birth.

The second observation about the inscriptions of the south iwan is that the mostly pious inscriptions contain Koranic passages, generalized formulas like *al-mulk lilāh,* "power is God's," Shi͑ite professions of faith with the names of the imams, even a verse of Hafez. What we have, in other words, is the elements for a Shi͑ite Muslim iconography of piety, mostly from the seventeenth and eighteenth centuries. As with the ex-votos of Catholic churches, it is the socioreligious context of a building's use which can probably be reconstructed through an eventual analysis of these documents. One example may suffice to show the methodological interest of the procedure.

Shah Tahmasp had put all around the walls of the iwan the first twenty-one verses of the forty-eighth surah (the surah of Victory, one of the most serene expressions of Muslim belief and expectation). Shah Abbas II removed verses seven to sixteen and replaced them with an inscription celebrating his own accomplishments in the mosque. This raises a host of questions about the evolution in value or charge of pious statements after they are put on a building. It is as though a pious statement, when put on a wall, is granted a period of time during which its meaning is protected and after which it dissolves into ornament. Or, a more distressing thought, it may be only after they have become fossilized that statements appear on buildings. They are there as mementos or archives rather than for their effectiveness. Obvious parallels exist on this topic with Christian, Hindu, and Buddhist architectural ornamentation, and an interesting, if totally unstudied, topic for religious architecture might well be the nature and duration of pious charges on public buildings.

I shall return to some further implications of this point in the last chapter. In the meantime it may suffice to conclude that the ceiling of the iwan is fifteenth century and that most of its walls were covered with Safavid statements which look like images with various messages. The shape of the iwan and therefore its dimensions were quite a bit earlier than its skin. Galdieri's soundings and probings brought to light many details about its construction and technical uses difficult to interpret within the framework of this essay, but essential for a history of building technology and perhaps for an eventual detailed chronology of the building.[15] Under the pavement of the iwan were found remains of columns and bases from an earlier mosque.

Behind the south iwan stands a magnificent square room, some 15 meters to the side and nearly 30 meters high (figs. 19–22). Its ribbed dome is set on a muqarnas zone of transition, itself carried by a back wall and a series of eight heavy and articulated piers. Italian investigations have demonstrated that this domed hall was erected over an older hypostyle area and especially that when it was built it stood alone, without anything abutting it (fig. 23).[16] Galdieri's reconstruction, even though based on a considerable experience of the building, poses several visual problems, not the least of which are the difficulties involved in imagining prayer in the proposed setting. It is most likely that this particular intervention must be understood as the brutal injection of a new taste or of a new function within the more or less well preserved remains of an older building.

The dome has two preserved inscriptions and several traces of lost ones. One, at the base of the dome inside, is a magnificent regal statement of power:

The construction of this cupola has been ordered during the days of the magnificent sultan, the august king of kings, the king of the East and of the West, the pillar of Islam and of Muslims, Muʿizz al-dunyā wa al-dīn, Abū al-Fath Malikshāh son of Muhammad son of David, the right hand of the caliph of God, Commander of the Faithful—may God glorify his victories—the slave eager for the mercy of God al-Hasan ibn Ali b. Ishāq [this is the celebrated vizier and theoretician of the Seljuq state Nizām al-Mulk] by the hand of Abu al-Fath the son of Muhammad the treasurer (al-khāzin).[17]

A complex argument based on the titulature of Malikshah, one of the most brilliant rulers of the Seljuq world, led Sheila Blair to narrow the dates 1072–93 implied by the names on the inscription and to propose the more specific dates of 1086–88.[18] This specific date accords wonderfully with whatever is known of the rest of the building, as will be demonstrated in the following chapter.

This proclamation of royal power is written in an angular style well adapted to—or perhaps compelled by—the use of bricks as letters. It is in striking contrast to an inscription in cursive which has been discovered on the outer northern face of the dome, the one directed toward the rest of the mosque (fig. 24).[19] Only a small fragment has been found toward the left side of this facade; its location allows us, however, to posit that the first six verses and then a bit of the twenty-third surah were found there. The contrast in tone with the interior inscription could not be greater:

The believers will win through those who humble themselves in their prayers; who avoid vain talk; who are active in deeds of charity; who abstain from sex, except with those joined to them in the marriage bond or [the captives] whom their right hands possess, for these they are not to be blamed. But those whose desires exceed those limits are transgressors. Those who faithfully observe their trusts and their covenants; and who guard their prayers; they will be the heirs who will inherit Paradise: they will dwell therein.

32

Here in the earliest remaining instance of the use of the more easily legible vernacular script, the majesty of power is replaced with very prosaic and concrete references to daily life for a good Muslim and curiously to sexual relations. Only two other instances are recorded of the use of this passage in architectural decoration, one of which, in the Qutb Minar in Delhi, is part of a transcription of much of the Holy Book, while the other one, on a mihrab in Meshhed, is more peculiar and so far unexplained.[20]

One can argue, it seems to me, that the reference at the beginning of the quotation to people praying is the operative statement for which the rest is but a redundant attachment. Alternately it could be proposed that the reference to sexual conduct, hardly a likely choice as a redundancy for an invitation to prayer, reflects some concrete event of the time, makes a highly synchronic point meaningless centuries later. As with the Safavid inscriptions of the south iwans, we encounter here another example for the eventual assessment of the long-range value of messages, religious or not, in a building. The point applies to more than inscriptions. Some thirty years ago Richard Ettinghausen noted the presence in the ornament of the upper part of the supports of the dome (fig. 25), precisely where they could be seen from outside, of stuccoes decorated in the third Samarra style, a style of decoration rightly or wrongly associated with the Abbasid capital. Was it just ornament here or a reference to an "imperial" pan-Islamic motif issued from and associated with the cultural and still, at the time, political center of the Muslim world?

It is difficult, if not impossible, to find out on archaeological grounds alone from where inside the remaining covered part of the mosque, a believer could actually see the south dome from the outside. But, however it was done, the opportunity to do so did not last. At some point new needs arose or old purposes were lost. The spaces between the cupola and the rest of the building were covered, and these inscriptions and ornaments disappeared from view or became hidden to all but careful observers. Archaeological investigations have not, to my knowledge, provided a sense of the length of time, even very approximately, during which the dome was standing almost alone.

I shall be briefer on the east (fig. 4) and west (fig. 6) iwans and consider them together. They are, in fact, respectively called the *sofe* of the master *(ustadh)* and of the student *(shāgird)*, as though acknowledging a special relationship between them. On a scholarly level, one reason for looking at them together is that, as assumed by earlier writers and now demonstrated by Galdieri,[21] they were originally meant to be alike, and the modifications brought to their supports—continuous walls in the western one, heavy piers in the eastern one—are the results of independent changes around the iwans. Secondly, even though their plan goes back to the same period as the south iwan, both of them are essentially, in their visible shape, late Safavid works of the seventeenth and, in the case of the west one, even early eighteenth centuries. In fact, the east iwan is almost entirely the creation of restorations carried out as late as the 1940s and 1950s, but these restorations maintained and copied a large number of older techniques of decoration and of earlier inscriptions, thereby giving to the decoration of the iwan some documentary value for imagining its character in the past. Finally, the two iwans are different from each other in the amounts of data they provide. The eastern one has much more data of very different types (ornament, inscription, titles) reflecting different times, but nothing to allow for even a tentative chronology. The Safavid period is richly represented both in tiles and especially in inscriptions throughout the western iwan.[22] Yet most of the information they provide seems to me, at least at this stage of research and interpretation, to involve the mosque less as a monument or as a building than as a repository of an almost infinite number of individual experiences.

Here are two examples. One is a celebrated square panel in the western iwan which is one of the most commonly cited examples of complex geometric ornament using writing (fig. 26). It is easy to argue that here is a wonderful example of a simple design rotated 45 degrees which acquires two separate values, one as a carrier of geometric forms filled with (by the time of the panel) antiquarian writing, the other one as a violator of the sequence of both writing and architecture by forcing one into rare contortions to read the writing. And one could argue that here is precisely the use of geometry which gives it the high status so frequently heard and read about.[23] In fact, however, the corner spaces contain the following rather undistinguished pious quatrain: "As the letter of our crime became entwined [i.e., grew so long], [they] took it and weighed it in the balance against action./Our sin was greater than that of anyone else, but we were forgiven out of the kindness of Ali." The central

34

square is taken up by the signature of one of the most active crafts-men busy repairing the mosque in the seventeenth century. Even though formally related to the angular style of writing on the face of the iwan and in fact much more sophisticated in design, this panel is nothing more than a "plug" for a local artisan.

And, speaking of plugs, in a small and narrow passageway (area 102) on the side of the eastern iwan, a wall panel is found which originally had 292 plugs of terracotta between bricks (fig. 27). As Giovanna Ventrone has shown, these plugs contain the ninety-nine names of God, references to the Shiʿite sequence of imams, and praises of all sorts.[24] The date of these panels is slightly problematic, but it is certainly earlier than the fourteenth century. Their Shiʿite character, however, is odd for a date that early in Isfahan, although a celebrated stucco panel of Linjan and a number of other examples attest to the open practice of Shiʿism throughout the region. Was this a sort of private meditation or prayer area reserved for a specific religious group within an ecumenical mosque? Or is this kind inter-pretation too contemporary and smacking of a defunct nineteenth-century ecumenical liberalism?

The further study both of the architectural changes brought into these iwans and of their inscriptions and ornament will certainly bring up dozens of additional questions of that sort. In ways that are still unknown, inscriptions and decoration have transformed the very fabric of the building, its basic architectural shape, into something quite different, into wall spaces on which a society exposes its piety in a way which is indeed unique. But to pursue these matters re-quires investigations which have not yet been carried out.

The last iwan, the northern one (fig. 4), is known as the *sofe-e darvish,* which I will translate as the "space of the holy man." Here again the visible skin and most of the structure are dated 1667–94 during the rule of Shah Sulayman, whose inscriptions are full of Shiʿite eulogies but also contain a wonderful admonition to "those who are full of zeal, who pray, prostrate themselves, invoking God and who are dear to state and government" *(mahbūb lidawlah wa al-hukūmah),* an expression otherwise unknown.[25] Here also Galdieri's work has demonstrated the much earlier existence of a long iwan on heavy piers. For reasons which are not entirely clear to me, Galdieri has felt that this iwan was introduced into the earlier structure later than the other three, but still within the same epoch.[26] And, of course, remains of even earlier columns were found under the floor of the iwan.

Most unfortunately, the northernmost end of the iwan could not be fully investigated. Its present configuration with a two-storied recess at its northern end called the *shāh-neshīn,* "the emperor's place," is a Safavid, if not Qajar, arrangement with ceremonial implications which are Ottoman rather than Safavid (fig. 28). Furthermore, the idea of a ruler praying in an area at the opposite end of the qiblah is hardly likely in a building with the dimensions of our mosque. On a formal level, however, this configuration is of a space closed at the end of the court, whenever this esthetic was imposed on it. It was certainly not the original function of the northern iwan, whose two massive bastions with an opening between them and whose porous eastern and western sides suggest a passageway which, like a funnel, channeled people through a narrow space before spreading them out into the mosque. We have here our second clue—related to the first one about the place where the southern dome could be seen— to the existence in the mosque of an esthetic other than that of a static facade in the center, the esthetic of a strong axiality and a well-defined direction.

BETWEEN IWANS AND EXTENSIONS

The covered areas between the four iwans are relatively easy to describe and to explain, except for one or two details on the western side. Located almost always on the spot of earlier supports, a series of originally circular piers had by 1970 acquired the looks of a refugee camp or of a place for the homeless (figs. 29–30). Endless patches, repairs, reconstructions, additions, and idiosyncracies without written record have altered the original shape of the supports, and their surfaces are as varied as they are at times bizarre, with cute leftovers from old buildings cohabiting with machine-made bores. The visual and psychological impact is that of a series of four irregular hypostyle halls with variations in levels which are sometimes difficult to understand (fig. 31). The ceilings consist of small cupolas among which the same anarchical voluptuousness rules as among supports. Undated and endlessly repaired and replaced domes range in time probably from the twelfth century (fig. 32) to ten years ago and show a range in quality and success that is just as great as the time span separating them. These hypostyle areas, at least the ones confined within the perimeter of the first mosque, are void of inscriptions, they are very limited in decoration, and they lack any sign of function or use.

It is easy enough to respond critically to what appears to be a hodge-podge of techniques used sometimes quite brilliantly, but often sloppily and without regard to the surroundings. But there is another way of looking at these areas. They are wonderful examples of the operation of an ahistorical vernacular practice which over the centuries cleaned and repaired the lonely covered spaces of the mosque. There is little point in trying to establish a chronology of the domes or of the transformations affecting supports. What does appear here is that, from some moment yet to be determined, the culture and technical competence of Isfahan built up and maintained the large space of its mosque in the consistent language of brick-derived forms.

The schematic consistency of the intermediary areas is broken near the southern dome and near all iwans except the northern one. Near the dome and the eastern iwan we are dealing with a series of adaptations between the newly inserted form and whatever preceded it. On the western side, two separate oratories were carved out of the mosque. One of these, the northern one, is celebrated by the presence of the dated (1310) mihrab of Oljaytu (fig. 33). The inscription is unusual for its beginning, "Sultan Muhammad," operative both for the great Ilkhanid Mongol ruler in northern Iran and for the Prophet. It also says that this mihrab was one example of the "additions to buildings *(mudāfāt al-ʿimārāt)*" ordered by the sultan. Whether this refers to his building program in general or whether it has some specific Isfahan meaning must for a while remain a question. Equally problematic are the stucco inscriptions framing the mihrab and its tympanon. They are not Koranic, as one would expect in the early fourteenth century, but contain *hadith* (traditions) about mosques and about Ali. Such a Shiʿite context ought to be later than Oljaytu's time, although it is true that 1310 corresponds to his Shiʿite conversion. The history and chronology of this area are further complicated by the discovery of fragments from an earlier wall which led Galdieri to a more sophisticated interpretation of the very complex inscription, to several Ilkhanid construction phases, and to a redoing of the superstructure in the fifteenth century.[27] The area to the

37

north of the western iwan is probably Timurid, with possibly an earlier facade on the court.

Although raising all sorts of problems about the transformation of a mosque, these changes are all within the clear rectangular perimeter which had been that of the original mosque; they can be interpreted as reasonable modifications of a fixed space. More problematic and in many ways more extraordinary are the extensions of the mosque beyond that rectangle.

One set of additions is easy enough to explain. In the Muzaffarid, Timurid, and Safavid periods discrete architectural units were built alongside the mosque and eventually more or less incorporated into it. The Muzaffarid madrasah is in the southeast; what Galdieri calls a *musalla* and I would prefer to call a prayer hall or masjid (because of the technical meaning of the word *musalla*) from Timurid times is to the southwest; and large Safavid halls celebrated for their original vaults lie to the west (fig. 34). The problem in each instance is why these units were built, or, to put it differently, what specific need or function they expressed that could not be met by the existing mosque. A partial answer is provided by a much more original "addition" in the southeastern area. Remains are found there of an earlier building truncated in its own southeastern corner by some exterior intrusion. What remains from it are odd pieces, a brick wall and a brick Koranic inscription of the Throne verse (2:256), both dated on stylistic grounds to the eleventh or twelfth century (fig. 35).[28] No function or use is suggested for this area in ancient times, nor is one apparent today. It is in fact now an oddly depressed area, somber and unkempt, like a useless remnant from something gone.

I have left for last the most striking and in part the most celebrated addition to the mosque. It is the north dome, popularly known as the Gunbad-e Khāki, "the earthly dome," easily one of the great masterpieces of Iranian Islamic architecture (figs. 3 and 36–41). It was open to the east and to the south and initially made an uncovered space extended to its south and partly to the east. Recent and very tentative observations by Galdieri on some large walls which apparently have now disappeared suggest the possibility that it was attached to some other building further to the north. Yet it can hardly be doubted that its location on the same axis as the south dome was of primary significance for its placement.[29]

Much has been said and written about this dome,[30] and its main

38

features are easy to describe. It is a square pavilion covered by a dome on an octagonal zone of transition. All of its parts are superbly proportioned to each other according to the universal principles of the Golden Mean. Its supports are articulated so as to reflect the structure of its zone of transition. The latter, with its richly outlined muqarnas, appears like the bejeweled base for an astounding dome whose ribs have formed a complex geometric pattern generated by a pentagon around a (probably) open oculus. The dome is decorated on the outside (fig. 41) and especially the inside with terracotta, stucco, and brick. Most of the patterns are geometric and their full description is still difficult to achieve for lack of detailed analyses and of appropriate drawings and photographs. The domed room could be entered from the south, the direction of the mosque, and the west, a direction which cannot at this stage be explained.

It is also a heavily inscribed dome.[31] Inside, at the base of the dome, in large angular letters in brick, there is first a Koranic fragment, 7:54:

Your Lord is God Who created the heavens and the earth in six days and is firmly established on the throne; He draweth the night as a veil over the day, each seeking the other in rapid succession. He created the sun, the moon, and the stars. All are governed by laws under His command. Is it not His to create and to govern (al-khalq wa al-amr)? Blessed be God, Cherisher and Sustainer of the Worlds.

Then follows: "The building of this dome was ordered by Abu al-Ghanāʿim al-Marzubān b. Kisra Fīrūz, may God allow him a good ending for [his life] in the months of the year 481/[1088]." The personage involved is best known as Tāj al-Mulk, the main competitor and sworn enemy of Nizām al-Mulk, who had built the south dome a year earlier. Although the inscription is the traditional Arabic, like the south one, in it Tāj al-Mulk uses his Persian rather than his Arabic names.[32]

Under the dome were thirty-two panels on which were inscribed the names of God. Outside, on top of the niche of one doorway is Koran 17: 78–79: "Establish regular prayers, at the sun's decline, till the darkness of the night, and the morning prayer and reading; for prayer and reading in the morning are testimonies. And pray in the small hours of the morning; an additional prayer [of profit] for thee; soon will thy Lord raise thee to a station of Praise." It is a call to prayer, but not to the regular, canonical prayers, but rather to additional prayers early in the morning. It is a message of piety over and above what is normally expected, and it corresponds in spirit to the message on one of the gates not far from this dome (above, p. 26). The south entrance into the domed room has Koran 3: 26–27:

O God, Lord of Power *(malik al-mulk)*, thou givest Power to whom Thou pleasest, and Thou strippest off Power from whom Thou pleasest; and Thou bringest low whom Thou pleasest; in Thy hand is all Good. Verily, over all things Thou has power. Thou causest the Night to gain on the Day and Thou causest the Day to gain on the Night. Thou bringest the Living out of the Dead, and Thou bringest the Dead out of the Living, and Thou givest sustenance to whom Thou pleasest without measure.

Several ideas and messages are thus found in or on this pavilion originally outside the mosque and now forming its northernmost edge. One is a clearly expressed relationship to the mosque and to prayer. Another is the proclamation of cosmic power through passages of the Koran which, especially 7:54, are not common on buildings and, when they occur, are found primarily on Fatimid buildings in Egypt. A third is an emphasis on extraordinary piety. A parallel is further suggested between ruling on earth (every passage has at least one word derived from the root *malaka*) and divine creation, between that creation, *al-khalq,* and the most common term for "being in charge," *amr,* whence *amīr* or "prince, governor." And all of this seems to respond to a message on the outside of the south dome calling to prayer in much more prosaic terms and, among other things, proscribing illegal sex. Something is going on here which does not deal simply with building a religious building we generally know as a mosque.

The area between the north dome and the north iwan was empty until a later date, usually assumed to be the fourteenth century, but this date poses a host of additional problems.

This long description from the remote first glimpses one gets of the mosque to its hidden internal treasure, a pavilion which was initially not part of it, has led us around the mosque and back and forth inside its complex covered or open areas. We have not seen everything. I have not shown every detail of construction nor have I read every inscription. But I have, I hope, brought out two characteristics of the Great Mosque of Isfahan. One is the extraordinary wealth of the information it possesses. Except in the areas between iwans, it is a building replete with signs, with clues, not the least of which are the results of the soundings and excavations carried out in the building in a manner in which archaeological logic and opportunism played equal parts. These data, including the absent ones, are of many different kinds and values, and each kind requires its own variety of academic competence or leads to its own set of associations with other buildings or with other data. It is, in other words, impossible to say that the masjid is a work of architecture to be explained in whatever fashion architectural critics and historians explain a monument. Nor can we say that the mosque is only a place for the exercise of faith and of pious practices. The latter no doubt predominated in my description, but historical, cultural, and esthetic questions or observations constantly led into directions other than the basic act of praying and the primary conditions for a mosque's operation. Is this richness of information and of questions unique? Or does it exist everywhere, in all buildings, for those who look? Whatever the answer, it is proper to conclude that the evidence does not provide a single, simple explanation of the mosque. On the contrary, its main characteristic is confusion, as dates are so unevenly spread all over the building, as Koranic passages deal with everything from divine creation to sex and alms, as several techniques and types of ornament coexist, as everything visible seems to have no original connection with what is under or around it.

The second conclusion confirms the impression given by a rapid overview of the plan. It is a building with a history and, before pursuing broader cultural interpretations or esthetic ones, it is essential to see whether a chronology can be proposed for it.

CHAPTER 3

The Chronology of
the Mosque

Up to now, I have considered the Masjid-e Jomeh of Isfahan from
three points of view. There was the view of the pedestrian walking
from one place to the other in the vast labyrinth of the mosque as he
senses changes in elevation or in the texture of pavements. Then
there were the roving eyes of the stroller recording his impressions,
reading inscriptions, and evaluating the quality or the impact of what
he sees. And, finally, there was the point of view of the more remote
eyes of the scholar at his desk interpreting a plan or an aerial photograph, flattened two-dimensional images transforming into a simul-
taneously visible painting the visually mutually exclusive visual facets
of a large three-dimensional building. By removing sequential time
as a significant variable, this last point of view is the most immediately
accessible and yet, at the same time, the most abstract one of the
three, the most unrelated to the actual perception of the building.

None of these approaches or points of view was exhausted, partly
because each one of them, like an object examined scientifically in a
laboratory, could be extended almost indefinitely to every known or
assumed staircase for a full assessment of movement possibilities
within the mosque,[1] to the last brick in some obscure corner of the

building, or to the detailed drawing of every vault. Partly, it is also that any one observer sees only so much, restricted as he is by his own acumen, his imagination, the curiosity or talent of his eyes and feelings, and his preferences or prejudices. Granting these limitations, I hope to have succeeded in presenting a unified complex of buildings in a manner that made the complex reasonable to the mind and to the eye, as a sequence one perceives, as a set of forms and functions one comprehends, and as a unique combination one recognizes in a plan or an aerial photograph. In describing the mosque according to these approaches, I dealt with two kinds of evidence. One kind comes from the building itself and everything it carries, inscriptions, decoration, and other often removable and replaceable signs. The other is the archaeological evidence uncovered by the Italian team from ISMEO, some of which is visible, but much of which has now been covered over and is only accessible through publication.

However partial or incomplete, this evidence confirmed the facts that the Masjid-e Jomeh of Isfahan was a building with a history and that this history was not simply a matter of an addition or of a repair here and there; the latter were not all cosmetic changes within a basically consistent architectural type. In Isfahan momentous changes occurred more than once within the very basic structure of the building as it was at whatever time the intervention took place, and at some point we will have to explain why some alterations remained, while others disappeared. But, first, we must propose a chronology for the mosque. To do this, we must bring into play a new set of data, the written record of historical and geographical texts. Here again we are helped by the relatively easy accessibility of most Arabic textual references in Paul Schwarz's *Iran in Mittelalter* and by the existence of two eleventh-century texts, one by al-Mafarrukhi, the other one by Abu Nuʿaym, which are discrete local versions of the pan-Islamic tradition of city histories. As usual, the references to the mosque in texts are not always what the contemporary observer seeks to know, and some of these texts pose complex and fascinating problems of their own, involving in particular the history of the architectural vocabulary or of visual perception in the past.

The recording of architectural details, elements of description or story recalled by a building in the Middle Ages, is so idiosyncratic that

44

only a thorough study of many examples can lead to worthwhile conclusions. I will simply propose a chronology of the mosque, justifying, when they occur, my differences with other scholars, essentially Galdieri and Godard, and fitting into the chronology as many as possible of the observations made on the building.

Thus the following historical sequence is proposed for the building:

1. In 771 or thereabouts a Masjid-e Jomeh was built in Yahudiyyah, the still or formerly Jewish suburb of the city of Jayy. This mosque became *the* mosque of Islamic authority with the transfer to it of a minbar from some earlier mosque in the area.[2] At a point not clearly identified in the written sources, the mosque also acquired a *maqsūrah*, a fancy enclosure reserved for whoever was in authority.[3] Why the center of Muslim authority in the vast oasis of Isfahan consisting then of a smattering of rich villages and of an administrative center was established in the suburb of the older Iranian town is not clear within the specific constraints of the Isfahan area at that time. But the pattern makes sense within a broader Iranian context, as the better studied northeastern Iranian cities like Merv or Samarqand seem frequently to have moved their urban centers from city to suburb and back to city again.[4] Why the Jewish quarter was chosen is also unclear, except that it may have been more urbanized than other areas. It probably was an active Jewish quarter as is intimidated by a story preserved by al-Mafarrukhi of a Jew who refused to sell his house, located within the space needed for the mosque, until he could get an exorbitant price for it.[5] The story is typologically interesting at two levels. One is that it explains something that appeared at some later time to be an anomaly in the mosque—in this case a fountain for ablutions which was unusually located. The story was apparently invented to explain this peculiarity. The other level of interest, already pointed out by Godard, is the story's latent anti-Jewishness.[6] This aspect of the story may well be related to a more complex association made by Muslims between Isfahan and Jews. At some later point Yahudiyyah was interpreted as a city built by Jews after the destruction of the Temple, thereby connecting the mosque to an ancient and mythical past.[7] A mythopoetic aspect of Isfahan, once the new city had fully coalesced, is also suggested by the numerous accounts which place there, and not, as

45

one would expect, in Khorasan or Iraq, the birth of Abu Muslim, the catalyst of the Abbasid revolution, or which associate it with Alexander the Great.[8]

Whatever associations may have been spun around it, we have a mosque with a minbar and a maqsurah which underwent recorded modification of an undetermined but probably minor character in 840–41, 851–52, and 920–21.[9] Muqaddasi, writing before 985 about things he saw considerably earlier, describes a mosque in the middle of suqs, with round supports and the very odd and at that time just about unique feature of a tall (ca. 30 meters high) tower referred to as a *manārah* on the qiblah side.[10] Its location is most unusual, and it is one of the earliest recorded "minarets" in Iran. Furthermore, in some addition or side track *(ziyadah)* of the mosque was a tree as beautiful as the proverbial *waqwaq* tree.[11] There is little doubt, it seems to me, that the mosque seen by Muqaddasi is the one Galdieri calls the "Arab" mosque.[12] The name is unfortunate, as it gives an ethnic identification to a type which is nothing other than the early Islamic hypostyle mosque (figs. 18 and 42). In keeping with an ethnically neutral position, I prefer to call this mosque MJ II, reserving MJ I for an earlier building found below it and at a different angle. Too little is known about this first building to say much about it, but it probably deserves at least an empty spot with a question mark in a Mendeleevian table of Isfahan's mosque history, inasmuch as it may fit with a still poorly explored problem with early mosques, which is that their direction was quite haphazard and that therefore adjustments had often to be made later.[13]

In addition to its unusual minaret, this early Islamic hypostyle mosque contained another anomaly uncovered by Galdieri's excavations which was destined to play a significant part in the later developments of the building. It is that the central bay on the north side of the court, the side opposite the qiblah, was wider than the side bays. The only explanation I have for this rather odd and, I believe, rare occurrence is that, from the very beginning, there was a north-south axis to the mosque, for reasons which cannot at this stage be elucidated. Otherwise one can visualize through details such as a pier (visible on fig. 29) covered with floriated stucco in the southeastern quadrant a typical rectangular hypostyle building, probably with empty tracts, *ziyadahs,* on the sides, as in Iraq, Egypt or Tunisia.

2. MJ III (fig. 43) is a Buyid transformation of MJ II carried out

46

between 985 and 1040, the later date being that of Mafarrukhi's text and not one determined by some significant event. Its features are identified from excavations, from original fragments incorporated into the later mosques, and from several literary references. There was, first of all, a new facade on court. It was built in baked brick, a distinctive new style of decorating surfaces with the material of construction introduced into the earlier Abbasid building from northeastern Iran.[14] Small fragments of constructions from this period outside the basic rectangle of the Abbasid mosque remain in the northwestern (199–202), southwestern (74, 65, 56, 43), and western areas (293).[15] They probably correspond to the four *adwar* ("buildings") bordering the mosque's *riwaq* according to Mafarrukhi and devoted to teaching, to a library, and to the accommodation of visitors. Their specific location in Galdieri's reconstruction is, in my judgment, more speculative than he makes it out to be, but it is based on the demonstrated presence of earlier fragments. Two minarets— our earliest recorded instance of the double minaret—framed a gilt doorway opening on the suq of dyers. They were standing on two pedestals called *fīlifā'*, "elephant's foot."[16]

Some of these novelties could be explained as natural or normal forms of growth to meet whatever new needs had come about or, even more simply, as maintenance. But enough evidence exists to suggest that much more was afoot than mere maintenance or repairs. In order to justify this interpretation of MJ III, it is necessary to sketch out what can be imagined or reconstructed of the history of Isfahan at that time. It was a period of considerable tranquility in Isfahan, in spite of one or two epidemics and the need to build walls around the city against real or imaginary foes. The same governor, Ala al-Dawlah Muhammed b. Dushmanziyar, ruled the area for nearly forty years, in those days a sure sign of success.[17] But what appears to have been political and perhaps even social tranquility did not necessarily mean spiritual, religious, and emotional unity.

The sign of considerably differing views within the population was the building some time before 985 of a second large congregational mosque under the sponsorship of a Buyid vizier. It was known as the Jorjir mosque. It is generally agreed that the facade uncovered some twenty-five years ago inside the entrance complex of the seventeenth-century Hakim mosque was in fact part of the Jorjir mosque (figs. 44–46).[18] From Mafarrukhi we know that the whole mosque utilized baked bricks, hardly known in the area earlier, that it had a minaret 100 cubits high (i.e., roughly 50 meters, 20 more than the earlier mosque), and that it included oratories *(masājid),* rest homes for the pious *(khaneqāhāt),* a library *(dār al-kutub),* schools for the poor, clubs *(majālis)* for the literate *(ahl al-adab),* and various other social institutions.[19] The remains of the Jorjir mosque are striking indeed, with their sections of spheres covered with writing and a desiccated vegetal ornament, and with their strongly articulated wall elevations covered with geometric brick ornament. Not only were all these techniques of building and designing new to southwestern Iran, but they were all outer-directed, projecting the mosque into its immediate surroundings through a gate and, with the high minaret, into the city as a whole. Why this mosque was built is intimated by its inscriptions. There are the common attributes of God, *al-qadrah lilah* or *al-ʿuzmah lilah,* "power or greatness to God," set in a proclamatory way absent until then from Islamic architecture. And there was a Koranic inscription, 3:18: "God bears witness that there is no God but He, and the angels, and men possessed of knowledge upholding justice *(wa ūlū al-ʿilm qā-ʿiman bil-qisāt);* there is no god but He, the All-mighty, the All-wise." There is need for a full historical exegesis of this passage so often used in heterodox circles as well as of the following verse which deals with those who have turned away from the signs of God *(ayāt Allāh).* In the meantime I will simply recall Richard Bulliet's study of many years ago which, through an unusual coin or medal, associated this passage during this very period with the Muʾtazilites, the more rational and philosophical wing within the great debate on the nature and implications of the Revelation which was splitting the Muslim world into sects.[20] In the tenth century, Muʾtazilites were often allied with Shiʿites, especially moderate ones as the Buyids were. A new mosque emphasizing learning and pious services, the externalization of the building through a variety of means ranging from high minaret to facade inscriptions, and the patronage of a Buyid vizier suggest that it was a Shiʿite establishment, probably patronized by learned men of rationalist tendencies, who would have used its social and educational facilities. The changes brought to our mosque, the old and traditional center, consisting of a refurbishing of the interior in a new style, of *two* minarets, and of *duwar* or buildings for various pious purposes, would then be a Sunni response to a religious and intellectual novelty and challenge.

48

The specifics of my explanation may be debatable or even wrong, for too little is certain about the sociopolitical, cultural-political, or ethnopolitical configuration of Isfahan (or, for that matter, of any city of the times) around 1000. And tempting though it may be to do so, the wholesale transfer to Isfahan of social categories proposed by Richard Bulliet or Roy Mottahedeh for Nishapur or Qazvin is not legitimate as such,[21] but it should be possible to develop for any city a hypothetical cultural-religious profile. It is also possible that both the Jorjir mosque and the Masjid-e Jomeh were simply reflections of a new taste, as happened in the seventeenth century or under the Qajars when the face-lifting of old buildings was commonplace without having profound ideological implications. All that seems certain to me is that, during the period of MJ III, the character of our mosque changed and that the changes were connected with some aspects of the life of the city. Whether practically, piously, or esthetically, the mosque's authority has been challenged and it responded with new forms. If I prefer to understand both challenge and response in terms of religious politics and ideologies rather than in esthetic terms of taste, it is in part an individual preference, but it is also my sense of the direction provided by contemporary texts for those feelings and emotions of the time which aroused passions and could have compelled architectural patronage.

3. MJ IV could also be called the first Seljuq mosque. It is in fact the only one which can be really connected with the Seljuq dynasty. Although it contains the most celebrated masterpieces of Iranian Islamic architecture, it was the result of a most peculiar set of interventions.

In 1086–87, Malikshah and Nizām al-Mulk, the Seljuq sultan and his most articulate and most intellectual vizier, introduced a large dome (figs. 20–24)—larger than any dome known at the time in the whole Islamic world—in front of the mihrab. It is a severely powerful, rather than elegant, brick construction which exhibits for the first time on a grand scale and with full attention paid for every proportion and detail the muqarnas zone of transition, a form probably of Iraqi origin which was beginning to sweep the Muslim world. Galdieri's excavations and surveys have shown quite conclusively that this dome was standing alone with an area open on three of its sides (fig. 24), but also that it was inserted into a functioning mosque. Most earlier theories, especially Godard's, assumed that an earlier mosque

49

had been destroyed or abandoned and that, at least for a while, the domed chamber alone was the covered part of the sanctuary.[22] Inside the dome a formal inscription in the by then partly hieratic Kufic script is essentially an official identification of the hierarchy of rulers. On the outside the beginning of the Koran's twenty-third surah in a more legible cursive is either an allusion to some specific event or person or else stands for the rest of the surah which is a fairly commonplace statement of Islamic principles.[23]

The second intervention in MJ IV occurred the following year, in 1088, and involved the building of the north dome (figs. 36–41), outside the mosque but obviously connected with it, all the more so since the dome was sponsored by Nizām al-Mulk's arch rival, Tāj al-Mulk. It is natural enough to see the north dome as a response to the south one. It uses the same new architectural language, but with a far greater sophistication. Its inscriptions are difficult to interpret, as we are not very sensitive to the pious or personal reasons for the choice of Koranic passages in medieval buildings. But the interior sequence from the creation of heavens and earth on top (7:52) to the value of prayer, especially of all-night vigils, through the thirty-two of the ninety-nine names of God, has a pious rather than a royal connotation. Outside, in what was probably a covered portico with an open area in front (fig. 36), we find 3:26–27. It is a rather curious passage which begins like a prayer to the All-Mighty and ends with a forceful assertion of God as the eternal ruler of men and of the universe (see above, page 40).

These verses contain a very rhetorically balanced statement about divine power, with, at the beginning, an emphasis on divine *mulk* or "rule," then an extension of that power into the creation of the universe, and finally the totality and almost the arbitrariness of God's power. It is possible to imagine that it suggests some parallelism between divine and royal power. The idea would not be alien to eleventh-century theories of power on earth, as expressed by Nizām al-Mulk or al-Mawardi.[24]

The area immediately in front of the dome was open to the sky (fig. 47), but in the northeastern as well as southeastern areas it is possible that remains from earlier *duwar* adjacent to MJ III were incorporated into the renewed mosque.

Two additional observations about the north dome ought to be

50

made at this point. One is that the titles of Tāj al-Mulk are given entirely in their Persian rather than Arabic form. The second one is a puzzle which can probably not be solved. Nearly all writers so far have taken the north dome as having a function limited primarily to its relation to the mosque to its south. Even though it was outside its formal space, the dome was seen as being part of the mosque. It was explained as a gateway pavilion, as a ceremonial chamber where the prince changed clothes before going into the mosque, as a library, and as an observatory.[25] A partial argument could be made for nearly any one of these suggestions, but not one is strong enough to carry conviction. And now Galdieri has suggested, but in a very tentative way, that, without denying its spatial and visual relationship to the mosque, the *function* of the north dome was related to buildings originally located further north and now irretrievably gone. Whether it was a gate or a pavilion in some other building will never be known. That it is difficult, if not impossible, to provide it with a function for the mosque is equally clear. It may be possible to argue, then, that this building is unique, that its purpose is also unique, and that its explanation can only come out of some external source, most probably a text, which would relate why a dome like this one was built where it was.

Such a hypothetical argument may indeed be true and is certainly valid to pursue, but, in the meantime, further refinements to an understanding of the mosque can come from reflecting on the visual and archaeological logic of the two domes. The south one is the first dated example of a rich series of large cupolas introduced into hypostyle halls or standing by themselves all over western and northern Iran.[26] Its technique, style, and decorative structure will be repeated in a manner that makes it reasonable to conclude that it was part of a type; perhaps it created the type but, if it did, the type spread so rapidly that it corresponded to a clear need ready to be implemented. The north dome has no model, nor will most of its technical and decorative peculiarities be copied or even continued. Even the intense logic of its elevation was not repeated, and its stunning five-sided brick ceiling design found no followers. Its choice of Koranic inscriptions is also relatively rare. The only message of the north dome which seems clear is that it responded to the south dome, both visually and chronologically. We are justified, therefore, to conclude that the building of the south dome, an early occurrence of a new fashion, elicited an extraordinary reaction in the city of Isfahan.

Why was it built? History helps a bit. The early eleventh century in the Muslim east witnessed the emergence of the Seljuq dynasty of Turkic warriors and sultans who moved westward from Central Asia and eventually, in 1055, took Baghdad. There they remained to become the actual rulers of the eastern Muslim world under the nominal authority of the caliphs. During this progression westward the Seljuqs took Isfahan in 1042, but for a period of some ten years revolts and counter-revolts plagued the city. During the last major siege of the city in 1050, the mosque was stripped of its wood, which implied that some of its supports—and especially its ceilings—had been destroyed.[27] Starting in 1051, however, and continuing until 1118, Isfahan rather than Baghdad became the de facto capital city for the Seljuq sultans Alp Arslan, Malikshah, and Sultan Muhammad. According to the chronicles, half a million dinars were poured into improving the city.

It is easy enough to understand the south dome as the consecration or the initiation of the rebuilding of the mosque under its new and victorious Sunni leaders. It was their royal *maqsurah,* their personal space in a holy place, as well as their way of glorifying the Prophet's presence. The size of the dome and its inscriptions proclaimed the glory and the wealth of the new patrons to the rest of the city. Several additional details, such as the coexistence of angular and cursive scripts, a moralizing passage from the Scripture, and possibly other details we no longer understand, served to strengthen the specificity of the dome's message. Over the following century dozens of similar proclamations will be made by dozens of local rulers in nearly every city of west central Iran through the medium of a dome with a sanctioned liturgical role, since there was a dome in front of the mihrab of the Prophet's mosque in Madinah. It has also been argued by some, following Godard, that these domes illustrate a return to traditional Iranian forms presumably utilized in pre-Islamic Sasanian fire-temples.[28] Too many arguments exist against this explanation, so popular in ethnocentric times, to maintain its possibility. We shall in fact never know whether Malikshah and Nizām al-Mulk thought of such a dome because the mosque was in disrepair anyway, or whether they destroyed an older hypostyle section in

52

order to erect this new cupola and to demonstrate the force of their Muslim faith or of their visual memories of and association with history. But, whatever the concrete and immediate reasons, the power of the final product is obvious.

The uniqueness of Isfahan, in this scenario, is that their action would have been understood as a partisan and ideological act and immediately elicited a response. It is even possible that the unique inscription on the outside of the dome contained a direct and specifically ad hoc message which was personal and pointed.[29] The response, whatever its motive, took a deeply pietistic form and seemed to cater to local ethnic sentiments. It was outside the perimeter of the mosque proper but, by its location and its direction, it engaged the mosque through that north-south axis created for unknown reasons in the very first mosque of Isfahan. And, most of all, the response was built in a hitherto unknown formal richness in which all materials available for decoration were employed and an elaborate geometry predominated.[30]

From the point of view of the building—of the monument of architecture which is the main topic of this book, the erection of the two domes in 1086–87 and then in 1088 has yet a different significance. The domes became the principal new foci of visual attention both inside and outside the building. Whether or not the tall minarets from the earlier mosques survived to this time is not known, but there is no reference to them in any text after the middle of the eleventh century, and no minaret will be built around this particular mosque until the seventeenth century, when the slender, decorative towers on the south iwan were added as ornamental rather than functional features. Yet, the eleventh through thirteenth centuries are precisely the time when Isfahan acquired a large set of minarets, many of which are still preserved.[31] They were not necessarily attached to mosques and most of them denoted a range of social and pious values. The minaret was obviously not the sign which indicated whatever the Masjid-e Jomeh was meant to tell, as it seems to have been able to do in the previous century. The mosque's message was expressed through the dome, and it was the message of the new power of the sultans so forcefully defined by al-Mawardi and by Nizām al-Mulk during these very decades.

Inside, the dome was renovated by the adjunction to its zone of transition of a new technological device, that of the muqarnas. It was then a relatively recently developed design process which transformed the areas to which it was applied into a multifaceted continuation of mostly spherical sections.[32] Uncertainty surrounds its origins, although a partial consensus places it in Iraq in the eleventh century. All sorts of ideological meanings have been suggested for the muqarnas, but the specificity of these meanings is still an open question.[33] We can be more secure about the esthetic use of the new form, whose geometric and other possibilities are fully exploited in the north dome, and whose irrational proportions based on the Golden Mean are precisely the proportions of the pentagon which generate the decoration of its ceiling and whose properties were being developed during these very decades, and in Isfahan, by Omar Khayyam.

What I am conjuring up here is the extraordinary phenomenon of a combination of talents, tastes, visions, emotions, and sentiments which centered on a single built ensemble, the mosque. Oppositions and antagonisms, mostly identified here in political terms, expressed themselves in one mosque, not two competing buildings, as they had during the previous period. The mosque became the space in which diverse powers within the same Sunni revival expressed themselves. This visibility was the result of a concrete time, a few years only, and the reasons why these particular years elicited that particular expression may never be known. For the growth of the Masjid-e Jomeh, it created not only the visual foci—the magnets—of the mosque from then on, but also its boundaries, its edges. They established the limits of the mosque's space, even if parts of it were not in the mosque yet.

The uniqueness of MJ IV lies first of all in the very specific dates —1086 to 1088—which can be assigned to it. This fact illustrates wonderfully the limitation of the evidence in our possession for so much of medieval art, East or West. Here is an instance where nearly all the *dramatis personae* except the builders have announced their involvement in a largely preserved monument at a specific time. Yet the building alone and the historical sources so neatly arranged in their chronological sequences do not provide a sense of the purpose or of the activities which would have led to the considerable investment, financial and ideological, in these domes. It is as though these stupendous constructions did not merit inclusion in the major chronicles of the time. Or, as is perhaps more likely, the order of discourse to which work in the mosque belonged was not the order of those who wrote and read the chronicles. To put it another way, the milieu

54

which recorded the deeds of princes, of religious scholars, or of holy men was not interested in or affected by the visual expression of some political or religious rivalry. Football and polo are not, in our own times, recorded in the same fashion in newspapers. For an understanding of the building, it is essential to understand these few years, and some document may eventually be found. In the meantime, all we can say is that MJ IV did not change its praying areas, but it modified the structure of the mosque by giving it new axes of expression and a new vocabulary of building.

4. I propose to call MJ V a difficult and problematic transformation of the mosque which is certainly later than the concrete event that led to MJ IV. It consists of a number of modifications which end up by revolutionizing the building, but a coincidence between a reasonable sequence of building activities and the data about history, functions, and events that are available appears impossible to achieve.

It is easiest to begin with Galdieri's reconstruction of a series of changes or interventions in the mosque. His position takes precedence over all earlier ones, especially Godard's, because his experience of the place and his wisdom and judgment are unmatched. In fact, his sequence does not differ that much from Godard's except that the latter introduces an explanatory theory for the changes before examining all the appropriate evidence. The setting of Galdieri's archaeological chronology into historical and cultural terms poses, however, a number of problems which have not been resolved by him or anyone else and perhaps cannot be resolved with the evidence at hand.

Galdieri's order goes as follows (fig. 48). First the south iwan was put in, replacing a hypostyle segment of the Abbasid mosque. For a while the iwan may well have remained unattached to the hypostyle on its eastern and western sides. The reason for the building of an iwan would have been to effect the integration of the dome with the rest of the mosque, to create a link between mosque and dome, thereby implying that at least part of the message of the dome was no longer operative. This would have been particularly true for the message from the Koranic inscription on the outside, which would have become nearly invisible. It is even possible, according to Galdieri, that the initial ceiling of the iwan was simply a wooden one, and not a barrel vault. This may have been no more than a temporary device, explainable by budgetary reasons, but the very possibility of such a mundane explanation sets a different tone to the interventions of MJ V.

The second step was the building of the eastern and western iwans. They are usually paired because they are so much alike in nearly all their original features including dimensions and interior structure. The eastern one probably remained freestanding for a while, which would explain the rather complicated links between it and the adjacent quadrants. The third step was the building of the northern iwan. Its different dimensions were the result of whatever previous use this area had, some of which have been discussed earlier, and it is particularly unfortunate that the full archaeological investigation of this iwan could not be accomplished, so that what exactly remains from earlier times is not clear, and the two heavy bastions at the northern end are still unexplained. But the most interesting point about the north iwan is that its side supports are not a more or less continuous wall, but a succession of piers. The explanation for this anomaly would be that the building of the northern iwan went hand in hand with the systematic but slow process of converting whatever was left of the hypostyle mosque into a domed one. It seems to have been easier to design the side walls of the iwan as a series of piers supporting side domes than to develop wall brackets or other devices to hold up the arches from a hypostyle arcade. A speculative but more interesting explanation of the northern iwan would be that it still served during the time of MJ V as a distributor of people who would still be entering mainly from the north side and that its openness was meant to facilitate movement in and out of the building. If so, it would admirably illustrate how flexible an iwan can be in accommodating purposes for its facade entirely different from those of its hall.

In the same period the mosque was extended beyond its original square in the southeastern and northeastern areas, finally achieving a facade on court with high arches linking the faces of the four iwans. MJ V thus ended up as a four-iwan mosque, a type which became common in Iran, but one whose meaning and origins are still much debated to this day.[34] Throughout the building, more or less meaningful links were created between clearly identifiable interventions (fig. 49).

Only two dates are provided by or for these interventions. A gateway was built in 1121–22 in the northeastern quadrant (fig. 16), certainly after the burning of the mosque (or parts of it) in 1121 by the heterodox Batiniyah sect. The fact that it burned down shows that it still contained a lot of wood and therefore that it was still mainly a hypostyle mosque. The second date is an *ante quem* one provided by archaeological evidence. When in 1310 the Ilkhanids built the oratory with Oljaytu's mihrab north of the western iwan (fig. 33), they replaced an earlier construction which was already bonded to the western iwan. The date of 1310 is not pertinent. What is pertinent is the general agreement that the Mongol invasions which began around 1220 stopped significant building activities in most of Iran. It is therefore unlikely that anything important would have been done in the mosque between ca. 1230 and 1310, and the area attached to the western iwan must be earlier than 1230. One more date may be thrown in before trying to propose an explanation for MJ V. The date is 1118, the year when Sultan Muhammad died. He was the last of the Great Seljuqs to reside in Isfahan. His successor, Sanjar, moved to the threatened northeastern frontier and died there in 1153; he is buried in a celebrated mausoleum in Merv. From the chronicles it is clear that Isfahan lost its interest for the Seljuqs and became a provincial city beset by religious and social strife. After 1118 it was no longer a place suitable for royal patronage of architecture.

This last point gives us a first clue for an explanation of MJ V. It was not a building or a monument created with a single purpose or ambition in mind. It was rather a building that responded to a series of functional needs and events. The damage from a fire started by what we would now call a terrorist group had to be repaired. The big dome in front of the mihrab had to be connected with the rest of the mosque. Separate areas for different sects within ecumenical Islam had to be accommodated—even the Shi'ites had their panel containing the names of the imams, though isolated in a particularly inaccessible part of the building. And a variety of technological means of construction, like, for instance, the covering of the south iwan with wood, were used.

Once again we shall never know how many such decisions had to be made, nor do we know who made them, but on the basis of evidence from elsewhere, the following scenario can be proposed. The mosque would have acquired a *chantier* with a labor force varying according to funds available at any particular time and with a group of possibly endowed permanent masons or carpenters. During my first trip to Isfahan around 1960 a small group was working on the floor of the court without any direction from government authorities and clearly without any connection to the restorers of the Department of Antiquities. There would also have been a committee of *ashraf,* or notables, representing each of the accepted religious sects, ethnic groups, or whatever significant divisions ruled Isfahan, which met requests, demands, orders, and types of pressure we can easily imagine, since they are found in urban life anywhere.

At that time, so far as we know, the Jorjir mosque had faded away, new mosques had not yet been built, and only small oratories in living quarters existed, marked beyond an area's confines by slender towers. The Masjid-e Jomeh had once again become the main mosque of the city, its place of congregation. But it was not a unified congregation which met in the mosque, but one whose sectarian divisions predominated. And it is to meet these varying allegiances within the same faith that, according to my hypothesis, a "committee" decided to build iwans which break up the unitary space of the mosque and allow individual groups to pray and to worship without mutual interference, as was probably the case with the Shi'ites near the eastern iwan.

Unwieldy, long in the making, probably never really finished, MJ V was the reflection of a new and different urban order, not very responsive to remote sultans or caliphs, but finding its own solution for its own needs. Except for accidentally fixed points like the gate of 1121–22, there is no way to date this growth, and it may well have gone on after the Mongol onslaught. Little is gained, I feel, in looking for Sanjar,[35] or for some other political hero, as the patron of interventions in the mosque after 1118 or so, for major political and cultural activities took place elsewhere and all patrons are not necessarily celebrated rulers.

If this reasoning and explanation are acceptable even as a working hypothesis, they have two major consequences. One concerns the common explanation of the mosque's form. Until now the transformation of the mosque of Isfahan into a four-iwan mosque was explained as just one example of a phenomenon known in western Iran beginning in about 1135–36, the date of the mosque of Zavareh, a small town near Isfahan. The phenomenon was the four-iwan type, that is to say, a theoretical standard that governed every actual

58

example. My reasoning about MJ V does not invalidate or contradict the theory, but rather suggests that Isfahan's mosque was not directly affected by it. It was an ad hoc solution to internal social and architectural problems, not an object created to fit with the esthetic, psychological or even ideological needs of a time. This suggests that, as in many other instances—for example, with Gothic architecture, or any major new type or style—diffusion from a single source is less likely than the collective discovery of the same visual response to the same needs.

The second consequence is that the madrasah theory, according to which changes in twelfth-century mosques were the result of the new teaching introduced by the Sunni revival, is also to be reevaluated. It too is not disproved by my explanation, but it is made unnecessary.[36]

5. A sixth mosque, MJ VI, can be identified as a fourteenth-century creation (fig. 50). Like its predecessor, it was not built at once, nor according to some master plan slowly fulfilled as funds or energies became available. It is, however, possible that further studies in the culture and ambitions of the Muzaffarid dynasty (1314–93) and especially of Sultan Mahmud who ruled in Isfahan between 1358 and 1375 may alter the impression of unfocused planning. What happened in this century seems, however, reasonably clear. In 1310, Oljaytu ordered the construction of an elaborate mihrab with a monumental inscription (fig. 33). It is a curious text which identified the mihrab as one of the architectural additions (mudafāt al-'imarāt) which characterize the rule of Oljaytu. The implication of this statement seems to be that the mihrab belonged to a whole series of architectural stamps put by the Mongol ruler over the sacred places of his empire. The point is that his work meant very little to the mosque as a building, especially if Galdieri is right in interpreting the ceiling of the room in which the mihrab was found as being of much later date.

Oljaytu's mihrab does actually inaugurate a new and relatively original use of the mosque, but it hardly affects its architecture. Later in the century, the area between the north iwan and the north dome was covered, a gate with pious mystical connotations built to the northwest, and the facade on court covered for the first time with a consistent decoration of muqarnas inside the iwans and of colored bricks and tiles elsewhere. For the first time we can be assured of a unified decorative skin over what had grown into a facade in spite of

59

itself. And, also for the first time, a purely esthetic, as opposed to functional, explanation can be given to this decoration. It is also in the fourteenth century that the two first additions are made to the mosque with the construction of a madrasah in the northeastern quadrant and of what Galdieri called a *musalla* and I prefer to see as a *masjid* behind the western iwan (fig. 51).[37]

It is probably dangerous to imagine what the mosque of Isfahan may have been around 1375 or 1380, but one would probably not be too far off to think of a space quite similar to the present one, with clearly presented activities corresponding to the requirements of the faith as they had grown in the fourteenth century, when religious teaching and mystical associations predominated over the formal expressions of power. The primary means of access were still on the northern side, with possibly a new gate in the southeastern zone, south of the new madrasah.

From then on the architecture of the mosque becomes a self-generating process in which outside intervention plays relatively little part. Repairs are needed as roofs collapse. Tastes change and affect the decoration of this or that segment of the building. New sections are built, for reasons that for the most part either escape us or still seek their investigator. In the Safavid period (fig. 52) the northern accesses seem to have been abandoned and eastern and western ones appear which correspond to some change in the history of the surrounding fabric. But for our purposes of understanding a building, the importance of those late centuries lies elsewhere. For them the old mosque of Isfahan became the shrine where treasures were hung, where decrees, laws, and other statements were placed. Real life may have been a mile or two to the southeast, but it is in the old mosque of the city, not that of the king, that Isfahan kept the rules by which it was run. From an architectural point of view, MJ VI completed the form of the building. From then on, only the elements that clothed it were occasionally changed.

CHAPTER 4

The Dimensions of
the Mosque

The chronology of the Great Mosque of Isfahan reveals the ways in which a celebrated architectural object came to the shape it had acquired by the late twentieth century. By "shape" I meant primarily the space it came to occupy. The reason for focusing on its development was in part because the mosque has an unusual shape within the "mosque" type, but also because of my own prejudice for history, for the identification of discrete moments of time and their synchronic interpretation, and because the "object" itself provides us with "time signs," that is to say dates and other chronological information which are an integral part of the building.

Why these dates are present and how they should be interpreted are rather complicated issues. For instance, in the interpretation proposed here, derived as it was from Galdieri's reconstruction, the south dome (at least its interior, which has remained intact) was a statement of royal or sultanic power and majesty plunked into a damaged or run-down old mosque. It may have contained some private, time-bound objective, but its main message, a dome in front of a mihrab, has no date. It is timeless within the perception of the building's purpose for users and patrons alike, for a dome in front

61

of a mihrab was an old form fraught with very Islamic connotations. On the other hand, Tāj al-Mulk's response, located to the north of the mosque, is very precisely dated, because the moment in history when it was built was an integral part of its statement, just as the date of the 1121–22 doorway was not put up in order to help later scholars explain the building's development; it was there as a statement of the time insuring that the damage done by a very specific group of rebels at a specific time would be remembered. Similar reasonings could easily be developed around the dates of many Safavid activities in the mosque, although by that time putting up dates and signing works of art or of craftsmanship had become more routine and perhaps a little bit less charged with meaning. These later signatures have led, especially in the study of painting, to an attributive rather than explanatory connoisseurship which has also plagued the study of Western art, even of the Middle Ages.

Leaving aside the particular methodological implications of the presence or absence of dates, the point is that the chronology or sequencing of time, as one perceives the mosque of Isfahan, uses the same date for two different purposes. On the one hand, the user-viewer-receiver of the mosque today needs a history to explain it to himself. On the other hand, those who built or intervened in the mosque sought at times to be sure that the moment, the time, of their intervention remained known, because that time had a significance of its own within their activity. These two-time data, the one the historian deduces and the one the building possesses within its fabric, sometimes meet and coincide, as they do in MJ IV and the activities of the late eleventh century or with 1310 and Oljaytu's mihrab, but at other times they are, if not at variance with each other, at the very least indifferent to each other. Thus the historian knows that between 1088 and 1310 a great deal was built in the mosque, that its forms were in fact revolutionized. But all the building provides by way of a date is the one on an excentric gate of 1121–22. The broad implication of this point is that one of the *dimensions* of the mosque of Isfahan is sequential time; this same sort of time is not a pertinent dimension of the Masjid-i Shah also in Isfahan or of any Ottoman or Mughal mosque. In the latter, both the visual perception of the buildings and the written information they provide argue for a single primary time of construction. The investigation of some at least of the dimensions of the Masjid-e Jomeh will help us in

62

providing the meaning of the mosque and perhaps in answering some of the queries raised in the first chapter.

One difficulty in dealing with the conceptual and perceptual dimensions of a building is that their definition leads to other buildings and to other areas much more frequently and more compulsively than the Isfahan-centered descriptions and chronologies mentioned so far. In other words, they extend the semantic field of our object and identify the appropriate comparative classes to which it belongs. Or else, the investigator constantly runs up against the absence of appropriate comparative information. In dealing with time, for instance, it would be useful to have immediately and succinctly available an interpretation with appropriate statistical backup of where dates are put on buildings and whether such locations form understandable patterns. But such lists do not exist, and consequently the pages that follow will be replete with identifications of topics for further investigation.

In addition to the dimension of time, the following dimensions of the mosque of Isfahan—construction, planning, perception, power, piety and society—seem to me to make up its meaning. I shall touch on each one of these categories, but not with the same completeness and thoroughness, because they require theoretical premises which have not been worked out, information which has not been gathered, or competencies I have not acquired. The last of these dimensions receives pride of place, for it is the piety and social behavior of Isfahan which, in the final analysis, explain its mosque.

With a small number of exceptions, where mud brick and beaten earth are used as in the old post-and-lintel-hypostyle (and perhaps even earlier)[1] and with the exception of contemporary concrete, the technology of building in Isfahan is that of the small baked brick. Historically it was introduced by MJ III, the Buyid mosque of the late tenth or early eleventh century. Within the accepted chronology of current scholarship, it would have been a novel technique coming from the northeast and Khorasan where it was already well established early in the century.[2] An alternate possibility would have been the Baghdad area, which continued or picked up a pre-Islamic tradition.[3] Some doubt may be expressed, however, about interpreting in purely diffusionist terms the appearance and growth of baked-brick architecture in areas from which it had been absent. It is possibly more likely that some technological and economic breakthrough in manufacture and distribution would have made the medium cheaper and more accessible.[4] It might also have resulted from the new wealth which came into the cities of western Iran and which would have allowed for this upgrade of the basic material of construction, replacing beaten earth or mud brick with a sturdier, if more expensive, material. Whatever the reasons, baked brick has dominated the construction of the mosque from 1000 until today, and there is not a surface, a space, or a corner which is not affected by the unit of building which, in Louis Kahn's memorable words, "wanted to be an arch." Nowhere but in Isfahan has this wish been better fulfilled, as arches (figs. 4–6, 29–30, among many places) and their extensions, vaults and domes (figs. 19–23) seem to have multiplied to the point where old and new, and everything in between, are almost impossible to disentangle. The overall impression is striking for its wealth and its variety. Furthermore, nearly all the surface ornamentation from the eleventh century onward, even including Safavid times, reflect directly or adapt themselves to the esthetic of the brick. The Timurid gate of 1447 (fig. 17) in the northwestern sector of the court with its esthetic of surface color belongs to another visual system and clashes with its surroundings.

As an example of Iranian Islamic baked brick architecture, the mosque of Isfahan contains two masterpieces of the late eleventh century with the north and south domes (figs. 36–41 and 20–24), and a few individual panels of the Safavid period with some originality (fig. 27). Most of what remains, however, belongs to what can best be called urban vernacular "without limit of time," to use one of Harvard's arcane terms for professorial appointments. What I mean by the term is the effect the traditional way of local artisans—without special orders or requests and within routine budgets available to them—had on buildings. It is a level of activity in which differences need not be explained in terms of time, of evolution, but in terms of bureaucratic financing or technological competence. In terms of artistic quality, the two Seljuq domes are not only major examples of technological and constructional breakthrough, but are visually powerful and exciting objects as well. Their very perfection raises the so-far unanswerable questions as to whether they could possibly have sprung out of earlier experiments known in Yazd, Tim, or Bukhara, or whether one must assume the existence somewhere else in the middle of the eleventh century of a particularly inventive architec-

64

ture which would so far have left no traces. It is easier at this stage of research and knowledge to assume that all of this was invented in Isfahan.[5]

Planning, the ordering of forms into meaningful and usable sets, is a difficult issue to deal with in premodern times and is a particularly tricky one in a building with a history like ours has. How is one to match a first set of conclusions reached by looking at the building with a second set derived from the building's history? Two examples may explain the problem. Galdieri's excavations established without the shadow of a doubt that the dimensions and proportions (1:1.2) of the present court were determined by the Buyid refacing of a traditional early Islamic hypostyle court. We do not know anything about the elevation of this last mosque, but, on the basis of the wider central naves on the southern and northern sides of the court and of comparative examples elsewhere, it is reasonable to assume a view from the court which was weighted toward the qiblah, whatever means were used to make this essentially north-south vectorial axis visible. At some point between 1118 and 1120, the centering of the monument was changed to the four-sided facade on court more or less as it exists today, but the proportions of the space used is that of the earlier hypostyle court. The iwans, let us recall, were built in at least three stages, and certainly no master plan was kept in some office in the building. A series of ad hoc decisions therefore created a successfully proportioned screen around a space first dictated by a different set of directions. But these decisions were affected by whatever was there before. It should be possible, for example, from existing but not available measurements to figure out how artisans determined the height iwans had to reach in order to hide what was beyond the screen. Answers to this kind of question would go a long way in dealing with the more insidious issue raised by the four iwans: did they derive from a type, that is to say from a standard form with predetermined or fixed sizes and proportions that could then be adapted to the individual buildings? Were they ad hoc answers to problems that differed on either side of the court? Were they logical growths from the modular structure of the early hypostyle?

We may be able to be a bit more specific. A peculiarity of Isfahan's iwans is that, whatever their common origin may be, they ended up by looking very different from each other. One acquired two towers (fig. 5), another one a goldasteh (fig. 6), a third preserved a screen with a good deal of ornamental relief (fig. 4), the fourth one hardly has a screen (fig. 3). Furthermore, they were all broken through in different ways and given different means of access to surrounding areas, but at least three of them acquired a comparable muqarnas ceiling, heavy and monumental, somewhat ungainly and bloated, but with a very important property. It could be seen from afar as the end of the iwan's space, it dominated and just about dwarfed the passageways below. The northern iwan, on the other hand, as a single deep tube, maintained its function of being a funnel, until once again a muqarnas-crowned concoction blocked its northern passage, but it is a vault which is hardly visible from the court. In all these instances except the last one, the muqarnas has become an instrument for the manipulation of large spaces. It was incorporated into the elevation of the court. The magnification needed to achieve this result may not be particularly beautiful or attractive, but, from our point of view of understanding the planning dimensions of the mosque, this use of the muqarnas illustrates the paucity of available models for a new vision of the inner facade of a mosque. The exquisite subdivisions of the muqarnas squinch or even dome so frequent inside buildings were transformed here into gigantic challenges to gravity, with the gigantic unfortunately predominating.

The court of Isfahan's mosque is archaeologically, that is to say from the point of view of its earliest evidence, a bizarre hodgepodge of decisions and interventions which sought to find or to keep an equilibrium between at least two incompatible pulls, a north-south qiblah axis and a central court. The result would have been as ungainly as the muqarnas of the west iwans if at some time either in the fourteenth or the seventeenth century (or both), color had not been introduced onto the brick fabric to unify its very disparate elements and provide the centralizing esthetic that it now has; but its symmetrical values are also only an appearance, as details rarely, if ever, match each other except in contemporary restorations, which have the tendency to introduce symmetry everywhere. It is as though iwans and color, the most obvious characteristics of the mosque's design, were but an afterthought, like a quilt thrown over aging or broken furniture. Of course, they *were* afterthoughts. The scale and the rhythm remain those of the hypostyle planned centuries earlier.

Another unusual result of the mosque's hypostyle origins occurs in the compositional module, made up of more or less four-meter

66

squares, which covers most of it. In a hypostyle the multiplicity of supports is emphasized by long flat ceilings on arches, which were two-dimensional coverings of space, with occasional "breaks," as Gombrich calls them,[6] for special considerations of one sort or another. Here, the domical system of covering identified each bay as a separate entity and either made the bays obviously repetitive, as with the Safavid repairs in the southwestern quadrants (fig. 34), or allowed for so many distinctions or breaks from the norm that there is no way of deciding how appropriate the meaning is for any one of them or for the space under them.

The location of the mosque's entrances is another one of its compositional anomalies. Each entrance can no doubt be explained in terms of urban development and of urban change, but in terms of the building itself they are extrinsic to any interior order except, once again, the early hypostyle order on the north side. We can only imagine that around 1000 two minarets flanked a gilt portal, exactly as they did at Yazd in the fourteenth century. But unlike Yazd, the entries of Isfahan from the fourteenth century onward were hardly visually important, and the situation remained that way until modern times when entrances were built on the southeastern side, the side of most frequent access today. Before that, one literally sneaked into the mosque.

Additional examples can be adduced to show that, whereas the constructional language of the mosque is reasonably consistent (with exceptions here and there), its design is far less so, and was for the most part an endemic attempt to provide visual and proportional order to anarchically disparate elements (or so it seems from a compositional point of view) brought for extraneous reasons into a scheme initially created by a hypostyle system that had not existed since 1100. The result is a series of formal paradoxes: a court which is also a facade; an elevation which harmonizes very different forms, especially iwans, used for different purposes; visual focal points invisible from most of the mosque and in one case, the north dome, meaningless since the twelfth century; locked and disused formal gates and secondary entrances; architectonic quality of domes or vaults and two-dimensional surfaces; and many others. It is possible, and it has been done,[7] to interpret these paradoxes as expressions of a continuous dialogue or conflict in medieval Iranian architecture between two different systems of architectural values, one inventive in bril-

67

liant three-dimensional compositions of brick, the other fascinated by the evanescent and constantly changing play of light on colorful surfaces. The two systems would in fact have always coexisted in the uneasy equilibrium necessary to the self-identity of Iranian Islamic culture. This sort of explanation may be valid and it is certainly attractive to popular national esthetics. But in retrospect, it is less satisfactory than one which sees the mosque of Isfahan as having preserved several episodes of the history of Iranian visual forms by constantly incorporating them into each other, like a quilt whose very quality derives from the incongruous variety of its components. Isfahan's success is the triumph of the forms themselves—dome, muqarnas, iwan, gate, court—whose flexibility and adaptability are indeed remarkable; it is not, like the Masjid-e Shah, an example of brilliant architectural design.

I shall be a bit briefer on my next two dimensions, the dimensions of power and of perception, because one is relatively easy and straightforward, while the other one is speculative and requires the elaboration of hitherto non-existent terminology of analysis. Power is easy enough to see in the hypothetical hypostyle mosque (MJ II and III) because the elements in it—a maqsurah, a minbar, minarets —were known to be signs of governmental authority. The two domes of Nizām al-Mulk and of Tāj al-Mulk (MJ IV) and the inscription of Oljaytu for his mihrab (MJ IV) are deeply permeated with statements about *mulk,* the physical authority of rule. But all these signs are old, pre-fourteenth century signs which, with the exception of the south dome, have lost most of their indicative value, because the spaces of their effectiveness—the open space to the south of the north dome or the area in front of Oljaytu's mihrab closed into a private oratory—are no longer there. And then, the Koranic messages from the early periods, when power and authority were involved in making the mosque, are now difficult to see, if not largely obliterated. In fact, the patronage of central authority was only really operative in planning and building the mosque until 1100 or perhaps 1118, when Sultan Muhammad died, and its only unusual contribution to the building was to have brought the north dome into a mosque scheme which did not need it. In the decoration of the mosque, on the other hand, dynastic or royal authority remains visible through the nineteenth century.

The dimension of perception could also be called the esthetic

68

dimension or the dimension of visual effectiveness. It is a dimension with two questions: How does one see the mosque? And where does one stop, pray, move, enter, or otherwise behave in one way or another because the mosque compels one to do so?

The reason this is a difficult dimension to handle is that it is nearly impossible today to live through or to behave according to the identified rhythms the mosque had before the seventeenth or eighteenth century. One can imagine walking through the 1121–22 gate from the bazaar and recall the horrible behavior of the Batiniyah shortly before that or, if one is a Batini, of the police toward them; one can imagine seeing the North Dome to the right and reading its inscriptions and then proceeding through an open space to a mosque whose large maqsurah dome can clearly be seen. But the size of it all and the originality of Isfahan's forms make it impossible to use the experience one can acquire of contemporary Ardistan or Zavareh nearby or of the large mosques of Baghdad and of Shiraz. A similar exercise can be attempted for 1400 or for 1700, as well as for 1960 or 1987 and I, like thousands of others, have done that, in the sense that we have all tried to perceive and to evaluate the Masjid-e Jomeh as it appeared to us or as our historian's habits have made us see it. But always, as I can vouch from the evidence of my own four diaries about Isfahan over a period of some sixteen years, I either deliberately skipped over some of the things I saw because I regarded them as inauthentic or new and therefore unimportant or else criticized the new for not being old. It was as though the mosque made it possible for me to be selective about what I could or should notice and how I had to react whether in feelings or behavior.

This potential for free choice of form to notice differentiates the Masjid-e Jomeh from Safavid, Ottoman, or Mughal, even Mamluk buildings of the same level of size and importance. In all the latter, changes in the original fabric—for instance rococo paintings in a Sinan mosque—can be ignored because they do not affect our perception of the building. If noticed, they are destructive of whatever form the building had. A Mughal mosque, an Ottoman one, and even a much more flexible one can be replaced by another building, but it is difficult to imagine them with incompatible forms added to them.[8] In the mosque of Isfahan, on the other hand, all changes, from additions of whole buildings on the outside to a new tile panel, can be fitted into the existing structure. This might have resulted in a chameleon-like structure, a Teflon style that could accept anything and wash it away or use it because it didn't really stick. But that did not happen at Isfahan, and the reason it did not came to me a few years ago in Palermo.

As I was visiting the Martorana and like every learned tourist admiring the fragmentary Norman-Byzantine mosaics, I realized that I was mentally eliminating from my purview all the late and gaudy paintings around the medieval remains. While I was thus acting out my profession, a few choir boys and a young priest came in chasing each other; all stopped for a fraction of a second to cross themselves in front of the altar and then ran out laughing all the way. They were at home in a church, and not maintaining works of art in a museum.

Since only a perverse individual would deliberately put something ugly in a church or a mosque, we must assume that everything, even some unfortunate restoration, is there because it was meant to enhance the proper use of the building, to protect it, and to increase the gratification, not of the esthete, nor even of the historian, but of the faithful. Whereas some monuments, whatever else they may also be, were meant to be works of art, the Masjid-e Jomeh of Isfahan was not one of them. It contains two eleventh-century masterpieces and a smattering of run-of-the-mill examples of works from the tenth (or even ninth) century until last year. But in contrast to so many of buildings from Iran or elsewhere, it does not seem to possess any formal, compositional, or decorative structure which would make it a unified and tightly knit object. And so much of its visible fabric is, as Galdieri has shown, a thin veil over old and disparate remains. At the same time, however true every one of these points may be and granted that it is impossible to reconstruct what it was like at any one of the times when it most striking features were put together, it is a powerful monument and it has affected many more people than the historians who can interpret and love the complexities of its history. Why is this so? The explanation lies in its dimension of society and piety. The explanation could be boringly called the cultural dimension or more subtly the dimension of life.

From the very beginning of this presentation of the mosque, nearly everything about the visible mosque made it different from most mosques in Iran and elsewhere and at the same time every detail, nearly every form, and almost every imaginable function has con-

70

temporary parallels in or around Iran. Only the north dome and the outer shape of the building appear as consistent exceptions. It is, in short, a stylistically, functionally, and formally coherent, or at least understandable, building, but one that differs from buildings with the assumed same function at any one time. Could it not be proper to propose that its function was not quite what is currently believed? The only existing parallels to the mosque are shrines like Mekkah, Madinah, Jerusalem's Haram, Meshhed, Najaf, Kerbela, perhaps Qum.[9] In all these places there is a continuous building and decorating activity sponsored by every level in society and meeting a variety of pious and social needs ranging from commemoration to housing or teaching. And then on certain occasions, usually under the impact of a royal patron, all these disparate creations are replaced, refurbished, repaired, or otherwise integrated into some new decorative or architectural scheme. Such transformations are rare in classical mosques. A small number of examples exist (Cordova, mosque al-Aqsa in Jerusalem, Yazd) where increases or decreases correspond to demographic changes and occasionally introduce new stylistic or formal elements. The Azhar mosque in Cairo has a very special functional history because it became a center for learning. The mosque of Amr in Fustat/Cairo is in fact the closest parallel to Isfahan known to me, and it does possess a special holy meaning as the first mosque in Egypt.[10] I am not aware of any holy memory or personage associated with the Masjid-e Jomeh of Isfahan and in its inscriptions or in textual references to it I have found no sign of funerary or otherwise commemorative significance.

What, then, is the point of these parallelisms with shrines? It is that our building-object contains enough unusual signs that it can be described as a shrine in a somewhat expanded meaning of the word, that is to say a space in which a precisely identifiable group enacts over a long period of time some set of consistent actions. In the Buyid period, ca. 1000, the peculiar circumstances of the time transformed a classical and perfectly typical mosque into the center of Sunnism. In the Seljuq period, two rival ministers with a clique attached to each one made the mosque a sort of visual and perhaps literal battlefield for what would have been a clash of ideas and of authority. But then, with MJ V, the slow transformation of a decaying hypostyle space with all sorts of adjoining spaces is accompanied by the following signs: near the eastern iwan a Shi'ite prayer area;

71

near the north dome a place for the all-night praying vigils used by Sufis; iwans dividing the mosque into what can easily be seen as places for the *madhahib* or whatever group may have been active in Isfahan. What was created is what we would today call an ecumenical center reflecting the rich complexity of Islam around 1200, when the strictest Hanbalites and the followers of Ibn al-ʿArabi or Suhrawardi co-existed in all major cities. Usually we assume that they gathered in their own mosques or in madrasahs devoted to each religious group. But is it always and necessarily so? Was it true of Isfahan? Perhaps even the existence of restricted institutions as early as the eleventh century does not preclude the common use of certain collective spaces. Every Muslim city would have had a topology of piety which would have affected its religious architecture.

In 1310 Oljaytu put up a mihrab with a formal inscription, from which the Koran is absent and whose top line consists of the words "Sultan Muhammad," one of the numerous names of Oljaytu himself, a most unusual ruler and patron of architecture. It then continues in a unique way: "This mihrab, made to be good *(al-mustatāb)*, is one of the additions to constructions made during the days of the sultan. . . ," and then a set of honorific titles and wishes for victories and for God to double his power. But the one who executed the job, a certain ʿAdud b. ʿAli al-Mastari, is nothing but a poor slave craving God's mercy and forgiveness. What this inscription does is to set in a visible but not particularly prominent part of the mosque an "image" expressing the power and presence of the remote Mongol sultan. It was not a functionally needed object within the mosque, but it used the mihrab, a liturgical and symbolic sign of Islam, to glorify the prince. What matters is the creation of what would have been called an "icon," if the term did not have improper connotations for Islamic piety. For this mihrab did not act, as an icon does, but it expressed the presence of a specific ruler, rather than of the Prophet as all other mihrabs do.

And from that moment on, the east, west, and south iwans and eventually the passageways near them became covered with texts and designs which deal with all aspects of life and contain references which we simply do not now know how to read. Why, for instance, is a passage from Hafez there? Some of these texts were arbitrarily truncated to make room for new ones, as the pious charge of reli-

72

gious texts seems to have a limited life, a point which is actually true of Christian images and ex-votos as well. And we even end up with certain designs used to proclaim God in one place and to advertise an artisan elsewhere. It is within this order of relationship to the mosque that its forms acquired names. The "earthly dome" (for the north dome), the "student," "master," or "ruler" associated with the iwans are all interpretations of a historical building by one or more cultural moments which no longer knew why the building was built and, therefore, provided it with their own meanings.

The study of this enormous amount of material still remains to be done by someone more familiar than I am with the fifteenth through seventeenth centuries, just as it remains for someone else to study the texts of any one time to find out whether the Koranic references in the mosque inscriptions were or were not commonly used in speeches, sermons, and disquisitions at any particular time. In the meantime I am simply proposing that the Masjid-e Jomeh became from the fourteenth century on (and perhaps earlier) the shrine of a city, the place where the community, whatever its components, kept a record of its operative practices and beliefs, where it gathered and behaved in the various ways required by its ethos. The Ka'bah had played a similar role for the Abbasids until the Qarmatian revolt of the tenth century, and it may be worthwhile to look anew at Cairo, Baghdad, and other major cities from the point of view of the possible urban shrines in them. Perhaps Isfahan was unique, but, perhaps as early as the twelfth century, the sense existed that it was outside the norm of mosques. The inscriptions of 1121–22 call it an *ʿimārah,* a "building," not a *masjid* or a *jāmiʿ,* "mosque." Tenuous though the evidence may be, the striking monuments of MJ IV may just have dislocated the fabric of a traditional mosque and made it a unique work of art.

At this stage I am simply turning the mosque over to historians of times other than the early ones which have been most documented, to historians of religion and of society, to literary historians, to historians of Isfahan. I hope to give it to them as a more legible, although only partly deciphered, document and as one which is in fact a true document, a sort of chronicle over centuries of a city's life with itself.

It is perhaps in the final analysis this symbiosis between the mosque

73

and the city which is most powerfully expressed in the Masjid-e Jomeh of Isfahan. Kings and sultans built or sponsored great works of art in the mosque, but it is the inhabitants of the city who knew then and know now how to come to the mosque. Unlike rulers, they do not need gates, only entrances.

Postscript

BY DR. EUGENIO GALDIERI

After reading the paper given by Dr. Grabar at the Hagop Kevorkian Center for Near Eastern Studies, I would like to convey to him
my deepest gratitude. I wish to do so not only because of Dr. Grabar's numerous citations and frequent, kind references to my work
on the Masjid-e Jomeh of Isfahan, nor because of Dr. Grabar's
invitation to write these brief notes, but rather for other reasons,
ones that are more complex and subtle, and that I will endeavor to
explain here, asking the reader in advance to forgive this paper's
autobiographical tone.

Dr. Grabar's perceptive analysis of this monument, "unique"
throughout all of Islamic architecture, confirms (independently, that
is, from its value as the first, true, interpretative synthesis) in the
most tangible and visible way the validity of the research method I
used to follow in the building's restoration, and has set the founda-
tions for future observations and speculations. It was in fact my
official duty to oversee the restoration and conservation of this monument, and this charge allowed me to enter the mosque at the end
of 1970, remaining there in interrupted stays throughout various

events until 1979 and then returning in 1982—that is to say I worked there before, during, and after the Islamic revolution.

Architectural restoration has in the past few decades drastically modified its rules, especially under the influence of the so-called "Italian school," but it has also changed its direction and import. Thus it is no longer interested in architectural cosmetics nor in stylistic rebuilding nor in a purely technical restoration; rather, it is now concerned with a complete, "three-dimensional" intervention, aimed at the cultural (and also physical) preservation of the building as a historical, artistic, and social expression. For these reasons a project in conservation should always be undertaken in an interdisciplinary fashion, and aided every step of the way with the specific support of the art historian, the historian *tout court,* the paleographer, etc. There are extremely few instances (mostly in the past) where one scholar was the embodiment, or a synthesis, of these many, often contradictory, disciplines, and where such knowledge did not result from human pride, but rather was the fruit of exceptional talent and cultural education. I can think of only two such scholars, the Italian, Ugo Monneret de Villard, and the American, Myron Bement Smith—both of whom worked in the fiery Iran of the 1930s, and, as it turns out, on the Mosque of Isfahan.[1] I do not need to evoke here the vast and diverse nature of the humanistic and specialized work of these two scholars, both very productive but with very prickly characters.

For various complicated reasons (unnecessary and too long to go into here) I was asked in 1970 to put aside my work and investigations on Isfahan's Safavid pavilions in order instead to concentrate all my attention on the grand congregational mosque. I had once visited this mosque very carefully with Giuseppe Tucci in 1966. Tucci mentioned then for the first time, as a remote possibility, that the Iranian authorities might entrust the mosque to us for a full examination; I had then toured it a second time in 1968 with a group of scholars from the Vth International Congress of Iranian Art and Archeology whom I had been asked to guide through the mosque.

The task entrusted to me, I immediately understood, was so complex and enormous that I risked being crushed both by it and by the giants who had preceded me: A. Godard, A. Gabriel, E. Schroeder, M. B. Smith, A. U. Pope, M. Siroux. How would I be able to approach a monument so "dramatic," so stratified, so permeated with material richness, with religious faith, with hope, with violence, with authoritarian rule? In what manner could I fulfill the task entrusted to me—so highly technical—while at the same time trying to understand, or at least to interpret, the hidden meaning of the building? There was only one road left open to me, that of the simple analysis, but carried out along the lines I had been elaborating in those years: "total immersion."[2] I was virtually alone,[3] lacking a specific plan (basing myself only on standard, humanistic knowledge of the subject and the environment); instead, I was full of experience derived from being an active architect—one respectful of antiquity. I therefore could only begin to question the building with great humility and patience, hoping that the monument itself would provide me with concrete answers, whose validity only others, not I, would later be able to verify in historical terms.

However, questioning a monument so that it will reveal to you its hidden past is a process which requires a slow and difficult immersion in the building's social and physical context; it means creating a process of identification with the culture and with the people who fashioned it in their era. Thus Dr. Grabar's evocation of such a suggestive image ("I can imagine walking through the 1121–22 gate from the bazaar") touched me as a gratifying precedent which recognized in effect my attempt at complete identification. In the preface to the volume on the atrium-palace of Ali Qapu,[4] D. N. Wilber wrote the following: "the experts of ISMEO quite literally got inside the skin of the seventeenth-century workman."

My personal involvement and identification with the Masjid-e Jomeh had a final dramatic acknowledgment on March 12, 1985: two hours after the tragic bombing of Isfahan I was informed by phone of the damage done to the mosque with these words: "emruz farzandat asib did be vasileh do musaq" (two missiles wounded your son today).[5]

I am here evoking all of these personal details to emphasize my awareness of the precise limits imposed on my work and also to stress the weighty reciprocity of those limits: just as I had not been capable of interpreting the inscriptions or of drawing on the historical-literary sources directly, so the art and architectural historians who had preceded me had not known how (or wanted?) to use an analysis of the mosque's structure—seen in relation to its architectural evolution—as an integral part of their analysis; and this occurred despite their numerous and often brilliant intuitions, despite the remarkable help of the archaeological authorities at that time, and finally, despite the semi-abandoned (and thus more accessible) state of the mosque in the 1930s.

The collecting of concrete and irrefutable data done in the 1970s was systematic but unfortunately not exhaustive.[6] Nonetheless an attentive examination of the data did immediately bear fruit, in both a direct and an indirect way. It pointed to a new methodology in research; it allowed for the discovery of a hitherto unknown building phase, of the tenth century; finally, it challenged some theories that, along with the stamp of time, were about to receive the stamp of an *archaeological truth*. I am here referring especially to the theory of the kiosk-mosque—already convincingly attacked by J. Sourdel-Thomine[7] and definitively demolished by the results of excavations at the qiblah sanctuaries of the mosque in Isfahan, and then in Ardestan.[8]

The monument, questioned at length and analyzed with infinite patience, did speak: it communicated a good deal of information that was made available to all scholars once it had been decoded.

And the first important interpretation of the data (enriched of course by a new and in-depth examination of its historical character) is precisely this study by Dr. Grabar—vast but precise in its historical significance with persuasive and fascinating hypotheses.

From Dr. Grabar's paper a new image of the Masjid-e Jomeh emerges, one decidedly different from the building still described by many scholars as a glittering, enormous *objet d'art*. It has here become a monument whose external aspect, along with its political and religious meaning, has changed over more than ten centuries of continuous growth; it is a landmark of the city, whose daily, minute recording of both the delicate equilibrium and the clashes between the Iranian, Islamic, Shiʿite world, and the "orthodox" Islam has turned into history—and where history has become stone, gesso, bricks, ceramics. Thank you, Dr. Grabar.

Notes

1. THE MOSQUE AND THE CITY

1. Eric Schroeder, "Seljuq Architecture," Arthur U. Pope and Phyllis Ackerman, *A Survey of Persian Art* (London, 1939), pp. 1007–9.

2. Lord Curzon, *Persia* (London, 1892), p. 40.

3. Pascal Coste, *Monuments Modernes de la Perse* (Paris, 1867), pl. V. The same emphasis on later buildings occurs in Ernest Diez, "Isfahan," *Zeitschrift für bildende Kunst,* vol. 50 (1915).

4. I am not trying to use directly and formally the notion of "dialogism" developed by Mikhail Bakhtin and popularized recently. But as I was refining my own approach to the mosque, I realized how much its study had been, in a circular fashion, regulated by interpretations of period styles derived from the mosque itself. Although the point may be a bit unfair and other usually practical and mundane considerations were involved, even the order in which Galdieri organized his archaeological investigation of the mosque derived initially from preconceptions about the monument. But his own fascination with the monument is easily apparent, and I am not aware of another monument of Islamic architecture which would have had that impact on its investigators. In the West, Hagia Sophia, the Holy Sepulchre, Chartres, and St. Peter's in Rome have comparable histories of relationship between scholar and building.

5. The notion of organic relationship permeates the most sophisticated explanation of an Iranian Islamic planning tradition by Nader Ardalan and Laleh Bakhtiar, *The Sense of Unity, the Sufi Tradition in Persian Architecture* (Chicago, 1973), among other places pp. 81 ff. A different and more practical as well as less profound statement is found in *The Architectural Review,* vol. CLIX (May,

1976) devoted to Isfahan. Since 1979 the focus of this sort of research and thinking has shifted much more to Arab countries with numerous publications in English, French, and Arabic.

6. While one can only admire the energies of the pioneers in the study of Islamic architecture in the newly opened Iran of the thirties (Eric Schroeder, Donald Wilber, Myron Bement Smith, Maxime Siroux, André Godard, among others), the charismatic Arthur U. Pope was both a catalyst for the spreading of knowledge about Iran and the disquieting champion of dubious causes, such as finding the origins of the Gothic in Isfahan. A. U. Pope, "Note on the Aesthetic Character of the North Dome," *Studies . . . in Honour of Professor K. A. C. Creswell*, Charles L. Geddes, ed (Cairo, 1965), pp. 179–93; and "Possible Contributions to the Beginning of Gothic Architecture," *Beitrage zur Kunstgeschichte Asiens: In Memoriam Ernest Diez*, Oktay Aslanapa, ed. (Istanbul, 1963), pp. 1–30.

7. Lutfallah Hunarfar, *Ganjineh-e Athar-e tarikhi Isfahan* (Isfahan, 1344/1966).

8. Most of the new ones were found in the course of the ISMEO surveys and restorations. See Giovanna Ventrone, "Nota preliminare su un pannello . . . della Masgid-i Gumᶜa di Isfahan," *Studi Iranici*, vol. 1 (Rome, 1977), pp. 85–103; *idem*, "Su una iscrizione seljiuchide della Moschea," *Iranica* (Naples, 1979), pp. 313–18. Other newly discovered examples as well as all previously known ones which are earlier than the Mongol conquest will soon come out in Dr. Sheila Blair's corpus of Arabic inscriptions in Iran. I thank Dr. Blair for having shown me her manuscript.

9. Eugenio Galdieri, *Esfahan: Masgid-i Gumᶜa*, vols. 1–3 (Rome, 1972, 1973, and 1984); hereafter Galdieri, *Isfahan* 1, 2, and 3. The first volume is an elaborate and essential visual survey. The second one is a discussion of the remains of an earlier mosque found by the excavators, while the third one is a collection of discussions, often very difficult to comprehend, of individual sections of the mosque with proposals for its maintenance and restoration. It is regrettable that some of the sketches are so lightly drawn as to be difficult to read and that scales and cardinal directions are missing in too many instances. Otherwise the third volume is a tantalizing meditation on the mosque by one who lived its fabric.

10. Without necessarily embracing its rationalism and aware as I am of the difficulties involved in transferring its reasoning to a specific work of architecture, I have been much influenced by the type of approach outlined by Jean-Claude Gardin, *Une Archéologie Théorique* (Paris, 1979), esp. pp. 175 ff., in order to define the actual value of any one bit of information.

11. Abu Nuᶜaym, *Dhikr Akhbar Isfahan*, S. Dedering, ed., esp. vol. 1 (Leiden, 1931), pp. 14–30; al-Mafarrukhi, *K. Mahasin Isfahan*, Seyyid Sellaledin Teherani, ed. (Tehran, 1932), esp. pp. 81–86. See also Edward G. Browne, "Account of a Rare Manuscript," *Journal of the Royal Asiatic Society* (1901), pp. 417 ff. Paul Schwarz, *Iran in Mittelalter* (repr. Hildesheim, 1969), pp. 585–624.

12. André Godard, "Historique du Masdjid-e Djunᵓa d'Isfahan." *Ahtar-é Iran*, vol. 1 (1930), pp. 213–82; vol. 3 (1938), pp. 315–26; vol. 4 (1941), p. 363. Eugenio

Galdieri, "Quelques précisions sur le Gunbad-e Nizam al-Mulk d'Isfahan," *Revue des Etudes Islamiques,* vol. 43 (1975), pp. 97–122. The works by Pope and Schroeder have been cited above.

13. André Gabriel, "Le Masdjid-i Djum'a d'Isfahan," *Ars Islamica,* vol. 2 (1935), pp. 7–44; Jean Sauvaget, "Observations sur quelques mosquées seldjoukides," *Annales, Inst. d'Etudes Orientales, Univ. d'Alger,* vol. 4 (1938), pp. 81–120; Richard Ettinghausen, "The Beveled Style in the Post-Samarra Period," *Archaeologica Orientalia in Memoriam Ernst Herzfeld,* George C. Miles, ed. (Locust Valley, 1952), pp. 72–83. O. Grabar, Introduction to Galdieri, *Isfahan 3,* pp. 7–9.

14. Actual plans of buildings are not known in the Islamic world before the fifteenth century, Gulru Necipoglu-Kafadar, "Plans and Models in Fifteenth- and Sixteenth-Century Ottoman Architectural Practice," *Journal of the Society of Architectural Historians,* vol. 65 (1986), pp. 224 ff. Little is known about the actual process of building major monuments in the traditional Muslim world. For a variety of approaches see Hans E. Wulff, *The Traditional Crafts of Persia* (Cambridge, 1966), pp. 102–28; M. S. Bulatov, *Geometricheskaia Garmonizatziia v Arkhitekture Srednei Azii* (Moscow, 1978); Ch. Ewert and Jens-Peter Wisshak, *Die Moschee van Tinmal* (Madrider Beiträge 10, Mainz, 1984), esp. pp. 80 ff. The latter deals with a totally different area, but has interesting hypotheses.

15. See below pp. 47–48 for a fuller discussion of this unusual building.

16. Discussion and measurements in Gabriel, p. 25.

2. A TOUR OF THE MOSQUE

1. These issues still pervade my own more general statements on the art of the period as in Richard Ettinghausen and Oleg Grabar, *The Art and Architecture of Islam, 650–1250* (London, 1987), pp. 256 ff. Appropriate references to Sauvaget and Godard are found there.

2. Galdieri, *Isfahan 1.* The survey is, on the whole, an excellent one, but it concentrated exclusively on built features, on fulls, and avoided voids and spaces.

3. An excellent example of the transformation of a building is the case of the seventeenth-century mosque of Lutfallah, also in Isfahan. Its facade on the *meydan* is by now often reproduced as a wonderful example of brilliant color on the exterior of buildings within the Persian tradition, but the whole facade is a post-World War II restoration. An even more fascinating example is the Alhambra in Granada, most of whose interiors are wonderful late nineteenth- and twentieth-century reconstructions. It is the latter which have created the "image" of the palace.

4. The only major exceptions known to me are quite recent and deal with Cairo and Istanbul. For Cairo, see Nezar Al-Sayyad, *The Visual Structure of Islamic Paths,* Aga Khan Program for Architecture, MIT, (1980), among what must amount by now to dozens of student papers from the whole world. Also, in a more general way, Oleg Grabar, "The Meaning of History in Cairo," *The*

Expanding Metropolis, Seminar 9 of the Aga Khan Award for Architecture (Geneva, 1985), pp. 1–20. For Istanbul, see Wolfgang Müller-Wiener, *Bildlexikon zur Topographie Istanbuls* (Tübingen, 1977).

5. Myron B. Smith, "The Manars of Isfahan," *Athar-é Iran,* vol. 1 (1936), pp. 313–58.

6. The obvious exception to this generalization is Abbasid Baghdad, the Round City, but it never worked according to plan; Ettinghausen-Grabar, pp. 78 ff.

7. The numbers refer to the vaulted zones identified systematically by Eric Schroeder for the *Survey of Persian Art* and adopted by Galdieri. They will be found on fig. 11.

8. Hunarfar, p. 146; Godard, *Athar-é Iran,* vol. 1 p. 281.

9. Hunarfar, pp. 157–58.

10. I saw the same passage used in Turfan (Tu-fu), in Chinese Turkestan (Sinkiang), on a mosque which had been desecrated during the Cultural Revolution.

11. Hunarfar, pp. 80–81; also Gaston Wiet, "Inscriptions coufiques de Perse," *Mélanges Maspéro III* (Cairo, 1940), pp. 127–36.

12. The last major overhaul of the court was supervised by André Godard and took place in the thirties, but locally supervised repairs continued to be made until the late sixties. Pls. 61 and 89 in Galdieri, *Isfahan 3,* show in what shape the building was before Godard's restorations.

13. Hunarfar, p. 122; Godard, pp. 245–46.

14. Hunarfar, pp. 86–104; Godard, pp. 256 ff.

15. Galdieri, *Isfahan 3,* pp. 29–34.

16. Galdieri, *Isfahan 3,* pp. 19–25; "Quelques précisions sur le Gunbad-e Nizam al-Mulk d'Esfahan," *Revue des Etudes Islamiques,* vol. 43 (1975), pp. 97–122.

17. Hunarfar, p. 76; Etienne Combe and others, *Répertoire d'epigraphie arabe,* vol. 8 (Cairo, 1937), no. 2775.

18. Blair, *Iranian Inscriptions* (forthcoming).

19. Galdieri, *Isfahan 2,* p. 36, figs. 13 and 68. Blair, *Iranian Inscriptions* (forthcoming).

20. Erica Dodd and Shereen Khairallah, *The Image of the Word,* vol. 2 (Beirut, 1981), p. 83.

21. Galdieri, *Isfahan 2,* pp. 35–36, with details in *Isfahan 3,* as, for instance, pp. 49–52.

22. Hunarfar, p. 105 ff.

23. The pattern is discussed by Keith Critchlow, *Islamic Patterns* (London, 1976), pp. 70–73.

24. Giovanna Ventrone, *Studi Iranici.*

25. Godard, p. 264.

26. Galdieri, *Isfahan 2,* p. 36.

27. Hunarfar, pp. 115 ff.; Godard, pp. 233–36; Galdieri, *Isfahan 3,* pp. 57–60.

28. Ventrone, *Inscripzione.*

29. Galdieri, *Isfahan 3,* pp. 25–29.

30. Gabriel, pp. 16–20, Schroeder in *Survey,* pp. 1010 and 1011.

31. Hunarfar, pp. 77–78; *Répertoire*, no. 2774.
32. Blair, *Iranian Inscriptions.*

3. THE CHRONOLOGY OF THE MOSQUE

1. Galdieri, *Isfahan* 3, pp. 60–64 and 80–83, has shown in a rough way the results one can reach with this sort of analysis.
2. Schwarz, pp. 585–624, for a rich survey of sources. Add Abu Nu'aym, pp. 18–20, who was not known to Schwarz.
3. Abu Nu'aym, *loc. cit.;* the maqsurah was first in the town or village of Kushinan.
4. A. M. Belenitskij and others, *Srednevkovyi Gorod Srednei Azii* (Leningrad, 1973), esp. pp. 143 ff.
5. al-Mafarrukhi, p. 83.
6. Godard, p. 218.
7. Schwarz, pp. 589–90.
8. Jacob Lassner, *Islamic Revolution and Historical Memory* (Leiden, 1986), p. 126. Schwarz, pp. 588–89.
9. Based on Schwarz and the two chronicles of Isfahan. Someday a full and complete comparison of these sources should be undertaken.
10. Muqaddasi, *Ahsan al-taqasim*, M. de Goeje, ed. (Leiden, 1906), p. 388.
11. Muqaddasi, p. 397; as with all texts, there are problems with Muqaddasi's information and the general point of luxury may be more important than the specifics of a garden. For minarets, see the forthcoming book on the subject by Jonathan Bloom.
12. Galdieri, *Isfahan* 2, fig. 4.
13. David King, "Kibla," *Encyclopaedia of Islam,* 2d ed.
14. Galdieri, *Isfahan* 2, deals with it.
15. Galdieri, *Isfahan* 3, passim.
16. al-Mafarrukhi, p. 84; cf. Lisa Golombek, "The Abbasid Mosque at Balkh," *Oriental Art,* vol. 15 (1969) for further comments on the term.
17. Ann Lambton, "Isfahan," *Encyclopaedia of Islam,* 2d ed., for an excellent historical summary.
18. Shamefully enough, the only discussion of the remains is a short description by André Godard, "The Jurjir Mosque in Isfahan," A. U. Pope and Phyllis Ackerman, *A Survey of Persian Art,* vol. 14 (1967), pp. 3100–3.
19. al-Mafarrukhi, p. 85.
20. Richard Bulliet, "A Mu'tazlite Coin of Mahmud of Ghazna," *American Numismatic Society Museum Notes,* vol. 15 (1969), pp. 119–29.
21. Richard Bulliet, *The Patricians of Nishapur,* (Cambridge, 1972); "Nishapur in the Eleventh Century," D. S. Richards, ed., *Islamic Civilization 950–1150* (London, 1973); Roy Mottahedeh. "Administration in Buyid Qazvin," *ibid.*
22. Godard developed his theory in many different places; last statement is "Les

anciennes mosquées de l'Iran," *Arts Asiatiques,* vol. 3 (1956), pp. 48–63 and 83–88.

23. See above, note 22.

24. Nizam al-Mulk, *The Book of Government,* tr. Hubert Darke (London, 1960). Al-Mawardi, Ahkam al-Sultaniyah, tr. E. Fagnan (Paris, 1915).

25. All these theories, except the last one, were mentioned at one time or another by one of the writers in notes 12 and 13. The hypothesis of an observatory was mentioned to me privately by the late Eric Schroeder. It is in fact an unlikely hypothesis, but, as usual, the direction suggested by Schroeder toward something unusual and unexpected may well be right.

26. Professor Robert Hillenbrand has been the official keeper of the score cards on these domes. See his "Saljuk Monuments in Iran," the last of which is in *Oriental Art,* vol. 22 (1976), pp. 256–77.

27. Ibn al-Athir, *Ta'rikh,* sub annis 442 and 515.

28. In addition to Godard's work quoted above, see M. Siroux, "L'Evolution des antiques mosquées," *Arts Asiatiques,* vol. 26 (1973), pp. 65–112.

29. See Sheila Blair, *Iranian Inscriptions,* forthcoming.

30. The conclusion that the North Dome's decoration is more or less without precedent is based on the dangerous grounds of silence and of absence of significant examples of architecture in Iran or Iraq during the previous couple of centuries. Matters are somewhat different in Central Asia, but even there dated examples are very rare. On the issue of geometry, much has been written about its theory, but little about the chronology of its various types, and too many of the conclusions reached so far are insufficiently grounded in cultural history. See M. S. Bulatov, *Geometricheskaia Garmonizatziia.*

31. Myron B. Smith, "The Manars of Isfahan."

32. Another topic without a study. Outside of manuals, the best introduction is Ulrich Harb, *Ilkhanidische Stalaktitengewölbe* (Berlin, 1948).

33. As an example, see Yasser Tabbaa, "The Muqarnas Dome," *Muqarnas* vol. 3, (1987), pp. 61–74.

34. André Godard, "L'origine de la madrasa," *Ars Islamica,* vols. 15–16 (1951), pp. 1–9. For a more balanced view with many new elements, see Edward Keall, "Some Thoughts on the Early Eyvan," Dickran Kouymijian, ed., *Studies in Honor of George Miles* (Beirut, 1974), pp. 123–30.

35. This is what Galdieri does, for instance in *Isfahan* 3, p. 44.

36. All this is not to say that there was no madrasah in Isfahan. One was in fact built by Nizam al-Mulk. I do not believe, however, that it had anything to do with our building.

37. Galdieri, *Isfahan* 3, pp. 72 and ff. and figs. 70 ff. The issue deserves an airing more thorough than can be given to it here. Further information on the fourteenth-century mosque is in Univ. di Venezia, *Quaderni del Seminario di Iranisica 10: Isfahan* (Venice, 1981).

4. THE DIMENSIONS OF THE MOSQUE

1. There are mud-brick walls barely visible behind brick walls east of the east iwan. They are popularly thought to be the remains of a fire-temple and may well be pre-Islamic.
2. The prototypical buildings illustrating Khorasian and Transoxianian brick buildings in the tenth century are the Samanid mausoleum in Bukhara and the Tim mausoleum; Ettinghausen-Grabar, pp. 207–24.
3. For Baghdad, Samarra, Ukhaydir, see Ettinghausen-Grabar, pp. 75–105.
4. I shall return to this issue in a forthcoming study.
5. Many years ago, the late Eric Schroeder suggested to me that, in his view, it was Omar Khayyam the mathematician who was behind the conceptual thinking that created the North Dome. It was he, after all, who had at that very time identified the various properties of the pentagon. Like so many thoughts and ideas spun around Isfahan, this one is unverifiable but attractive.
6. E. H. Gombrich, *The Sense of Order* (Ithaca, 1979), pp. 110 ff.
7. O. Grabar, "Isfahan as a Mirror of Persian Architecture," R. Ettinghausen and E. Yarshater, eds., *Highlights of Persian Art,* (Boulder, 1979), pp. 213–42.
8. The issue here can be called one of mutability of forms. It is easy to see how a dome-centered building, like Sinan's work or St. Peter's, cannot be easily modified. But why is it also true of the Ibn Tulun mosque and not of Cordova's?
9. There are no studies of Muslim shrines, and for further information one has to go to basic sources; for these it is simplest to start with the *Encyclopaedia of Islam* and the major surveys of written sources. Some help should also be provided by the publication of *waqf* documents from Isfahan, Abd al-Husayn Sipanta, *Ta'rikhcheh Awqaf Isfahan* (Tehran, 1347). The waqf on our mosque gives no useful information for its architecture.
10. For all these mosques, see Ettinghausen-Grabar and the older volumes of K. A. C. Creswell, *Early Muslim Architecture,* 25 vols. (Oxford, 1959).

POSTSCRIPT

1. Basing himself on the oldest vaults in the mosque, Monneret had begun to face the problem of the cross-ribbing in vaults. See Pope and Ackerman, pp. 959, 960, 961, 1032, 1033, 1286, and the drawings corresponding to the vaults, nos. 42, 47, 48, 60, 61, 62. I also dealt with the subject in a Festschrift in memoriam of Monneret de Villard: "Contributi alla conoscenza delle strutture a nervature incrociate," *Rivista degli Studi Orientali, Universita di Roma,* vol. 57 (Rome, 1985), 61–67. I have retained an indirect but sharp memory of M. B. Smith and of his great love of the Jomeh mosque. During a long correspondence with his widow in an attempt to discover the elevation drawings done in the 1930s, Mrs. Katharine Bement Smith kindly informed me (1974–75) of her husband's

regret at having to leave Iran, and at running into embittered conflict with some American and French colleagues; that regret, his widow wrote me, had been lessened only by the news he used to receive "about the good work accomplished by the staff of ISMEO." Moreover, he had also expressed his great faith in an official manner in the 1969 December report that he sent to the UNESCO a few months before his death.

2. See the recent article: Eugenio Galdieri, "Il mondo orientale di fronte ai problemi del restauro," *Bolletino d'Arte*, vol. 71 (1986), 23–26.

3. Only after a year did the archaeologist Professor U. Scerrato reach the mosque at my request. From the beginning, however, the work of the archaeologists was directed towards an autonomous examination of the subterranean vaults, in a search for the primitive mosque. Thus a specialist's necessary and desirable control and corroboration were lacking during the restoration work. The highly acclaimed findings of the archaeological *équipe* between 1973 and 1977 are still awaiting a worthy and complete publication, and until now only a few sparse notices about their difficult and splendid job have circulated.

4. See Eugenio Galdieri, *Esfahan: Ali Qapu. An Architectural Survey*, (Rome, 1979).

5. One of the two missiles that fell on that area caused approximately two hundred deaths around the adjacent bazaar, totally destroyed twelve vaults and damaged another twelve, destroyed all the area southeast of the mosque mostly of the Seljuq period. The reconstruction project, despite political pressure for a rapid and superficial reparation, was executed with great care and ability by the local superintendence and by many volunteers, as I was personally able to note in an on-site investigation of March 11, 1986.

6. I have not yet lost hope of returning for a long stretch of time to Isfahan, to complete the research, finish the most delicate operations of static restoration and publish a last volume. Negotiations are underway for the translation of my third volume into Farsi, since the other two have already come out in an edition by the Sazeman-e Melli Efazat-e Asar-e Bastani-ye Iran. Recently my program for the completion of this study was made known to the public in a review published in France. See *Abstracta Iranica*, C. Adle, ed., vol. 9 (1986), p. 135.

7. Janine Sourdel-Thomine, "La Mosquée et la Madrasa," *Cahiers de civilisation medievale*, vol. 12 (1970), no. 2, p. 102.

8. A. B. Shirazy, "Masgid-e gamʿeh-ye Ardestan," *Asar*, vol 1, no. 1 (Teheran, 1359), pp. 5–51.

86

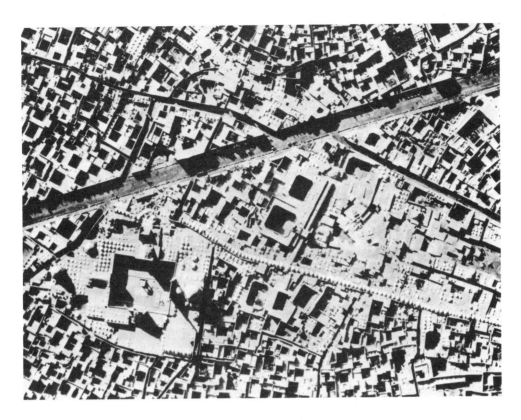

1. Air view of the Great Mosque. This almost direct view neutralizes contrasts between buildings of different heights or texture, but provides a reasonable impression of two-dimensional grids. On this photograph, south is more or less toward the lower part of the image, slightly to the right of the qiblah or direction of prayer. The areas to the south and southwest of the mosque show the long and narrow covered commercial street connecting the Great Mosque to the later Safavid ensemble, a few caravanserais and houses as well as recently pierced avenues.

2. Air view from the northeast. The more oblique angle allows for a more effective sense of vertical dimensions. This photograph is much later than the preceding one, as it shows the partial clearing of the area in front of the 1803–4 gate (see p. 25) which serves as the main entrance to the mosque.

3. Court façade, toward north; like the following three, this photograph was taken ca. 1960, i.e., before the east set of restorations but after the repairs and rebuildings of the thirties and forties.

4. Court facade, toward east (after Galdieri).

5. Court facade, toward south.

6. Court facade, toward west (after Rigamonti).

7. Roof in southeast quadrant (after Galdieri).

8. West iwan from the outside (after Galdieri).

9. North dome, interior.

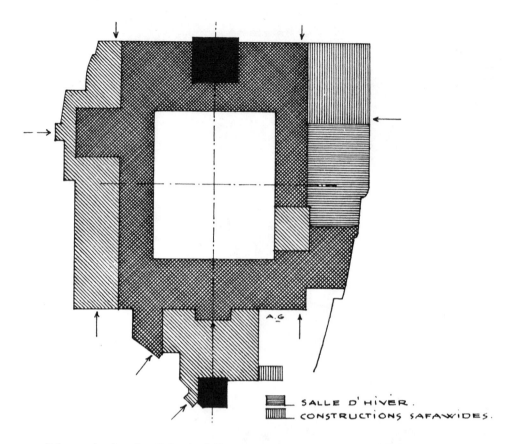

SALLE D'HIVER.

CONSTRUCTIONS SAFAWIDES.

10. Schematic sketch of the building's history (after Godard). The arrows represent entrances. Note how the schema has almost reduced a building to ashes.

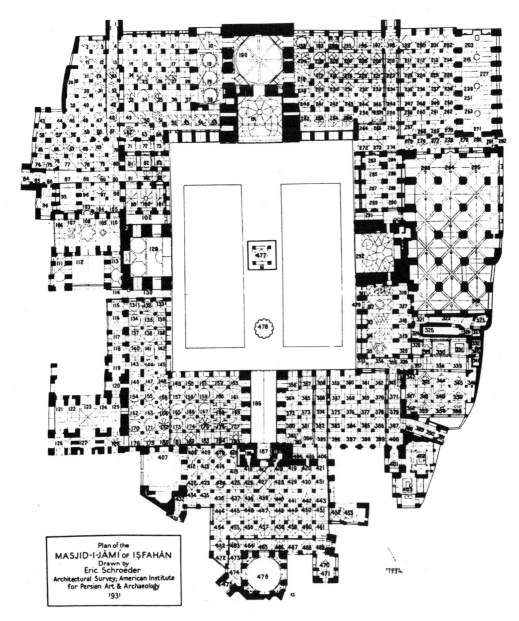

Plan of the
MASJID-I-JÁMÍ of IŞFAHÁN
Drawn by
Eric Schroeder
Architectural Survey; American Institute
for Persian Art & Archaeology
1931

11. Plan of the mosque (after Schroeder). The numbers refer to the numbering of the mosque's domes developed by Schroeder and followed by Galdieri; they are used in this book for the identification of various spaces of the mosque. In the text, I have conventionally designated the qiblah (upper part of plan) wall as south and all other sides accordingly. In reality the mosque is, incorrectly, oriented toward the southwest.

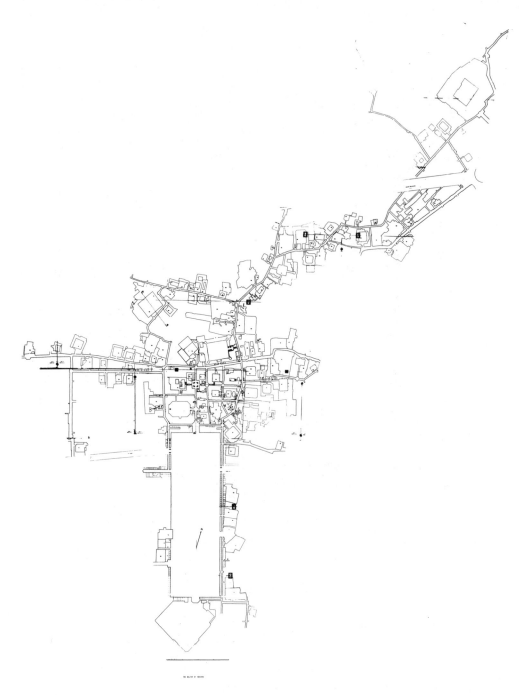

12. Plan of the area of Isfahan located between the Safavid ensembles of the seventeenth century on the left and our mosque on the right. Although often discussed and often reproduced, the rationale for the layout of this path (as opposed to its function) has not yet been worked out.

13. Exterior walls to the south of the mosque (after Rigamonti).

14. Gate dated 1366 and located at the north side of the mosque (area 475). The photograph is from the Herzfeld Archives and antedates all twentieth-century repairs to the mosque. It shows the gate as still in use and the surrounding area as barren of activities (Courtesy of Herzfeld Archives, Freer Gallery of Art).

15. Gate dated 1121–22 and located at the north side of the mosque (area 433). This photograph, also from the Herzfeld Archives, shows the gate in considerable disrepair (Courtesy of Herzfeld, Freer Gallery of Art).

16. Gate in courtyard (area 479) dated 1447 (after Galdieri). Both its location and its purpose are problematic. It may have been moved into its present location from elsewhere.

17. Detailed view of southeastern area; early column reset in later masonry.

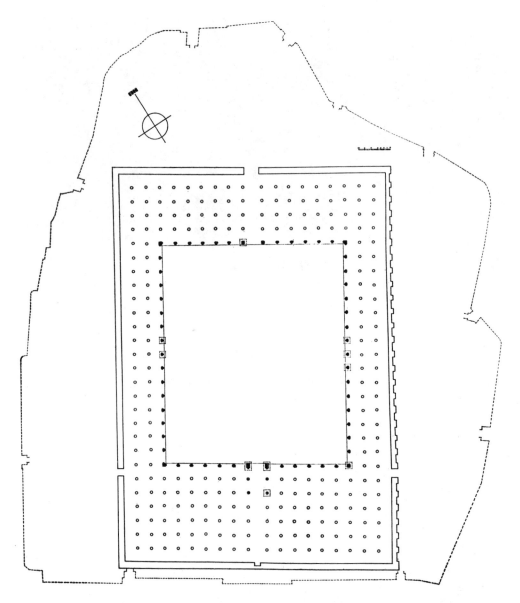

18. Plan of Buyid mosque after its second phase (after Galdieri); the explanation of the plan is provided in Chapter 3.

19. South dome, from the roof of the mosque.

20. South dome, interior toward mihrab, before restorations (after Rigamonti).

21. South dome, zone of transition and cupola (after Galdieri).

22. South dome, detail of muqarnas zone of transition (after Galdieri).

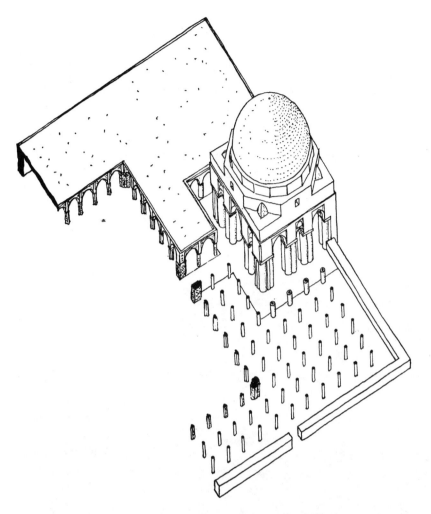

23. South dome, its position within the older building (after Galdieri).

109

24. Fragment of inscription (Koran 23:6) on north face of south dome (after Galdieri).

25. Detail of stucco decoration on upper part of piers supporting south dome. The motif seems related to the central Abbasid style known as Samarra III.

26. Tile panel in western iwan, seventeenth century.

27. Panel in area 102 with names of God and Shi'ite formulas (after Galdieri).

28. North iwan, back wall of indeterminate date (Courtesy of Herzfeld Archives, Freer Gallery of Art).

29. General view of covered area in southeastern quadrant (after Galdieri); note the variety of styles of supports.

30. General view of covered area in southeastern quadrant (after Rigamonti).
Note the wobbly look of constantly rebuilt supports.

31. Northwestern quadrant adjacent to north iwan. Note the various floors and the traces of all sorts of uses in the stucco covering piles.

32. Example of a dome (probably dating from the twelfth century) which was often repaired.

33. Area 312; the mihrab of Oljaytu dated 1310 (after Galdieri).

34. Safavid vaults in area 296–302 (after Galdieri).

35. Fragment of a brick inscription (surah 2:255) in area 20 (after Galdieri).

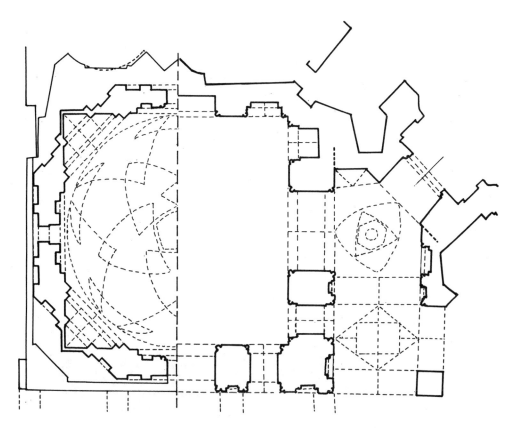

36. North dome, plan at 1.5 meters above floor (left) and 9 meters above (after Galdieri).

37. North dome, elevation toward south, showing the little planned way in which the dome was eventually connected to the rest of the mosque (hatching) (after Galdieri).

122

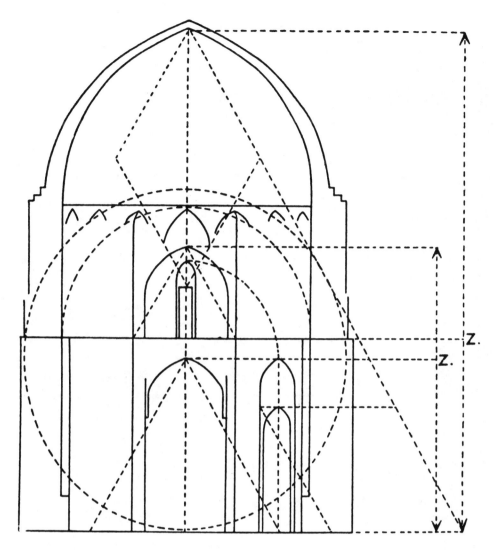

38. North dome, section; the plan and elevation of the building were composed according to the irrational proportions of the Golden Mean.

39. North dome, detail of muqarnas squinch (after Galdieri).

40. North dome, cupola with its extraordinary and still unexplained design based on the pentagon (after Rigamonti).

41. North dome, exterior.

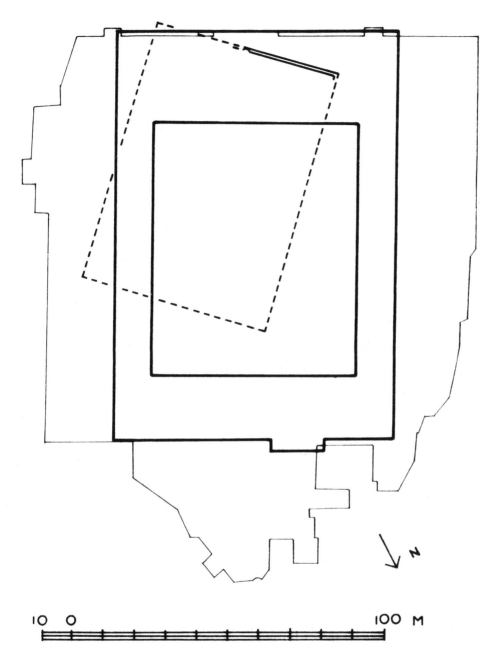

10 0   100 M

42. Sketch of MJ I and II (after Galdieri).

127

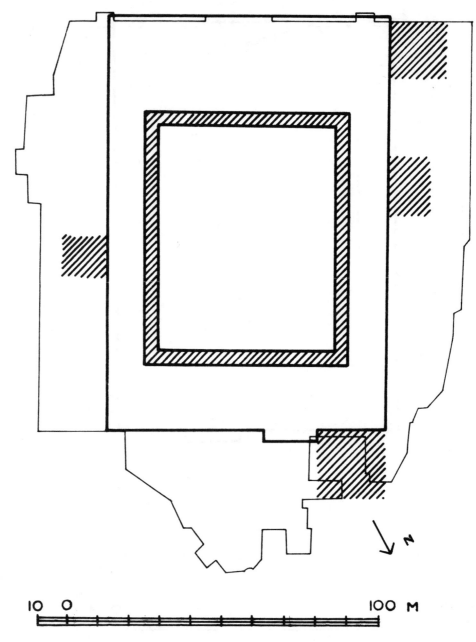

43. Sketch plan of MJ III (after Galdieri).

128

44. Jorjir Mosque, facade; note the articulated projection on the street.

45. Jorjir Mosque, upper part of entrance.

46. Jorjir Mosque, detail of squinch and side panels.

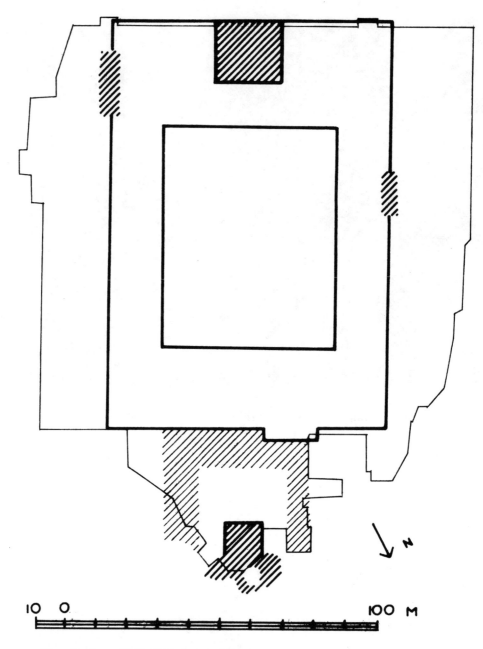

10 0   100 M

47. Sketch plan of MJ IV (after Galdieri).

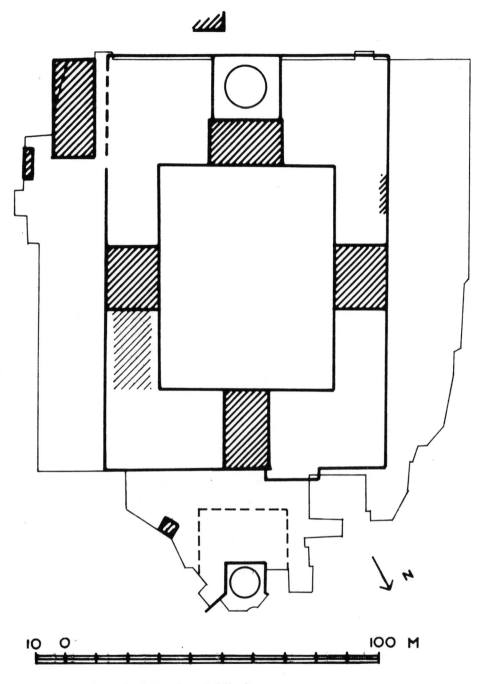

10 0 ⊢─────────────────────────────────────┤ 100 M

48. Sketch plan of MJ V (after Galdieri).

133

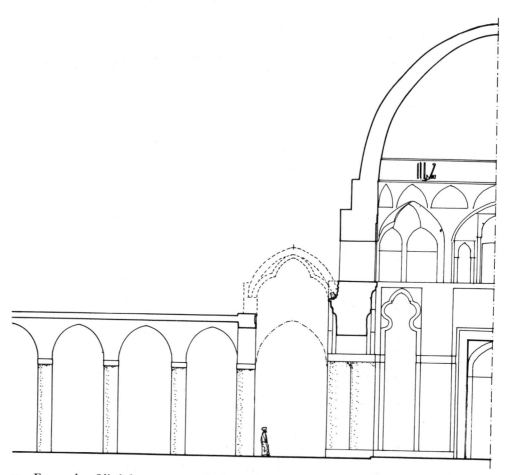

49. Example of link between south dome and surrounding hypostyle (after Galdieri).

134

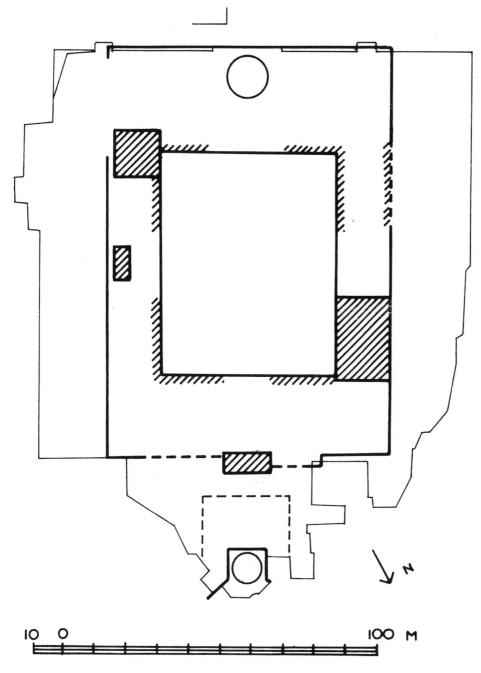

10 0   100 M

50. Sketch plan of MJ VI, first phase (after Galdieri).

135

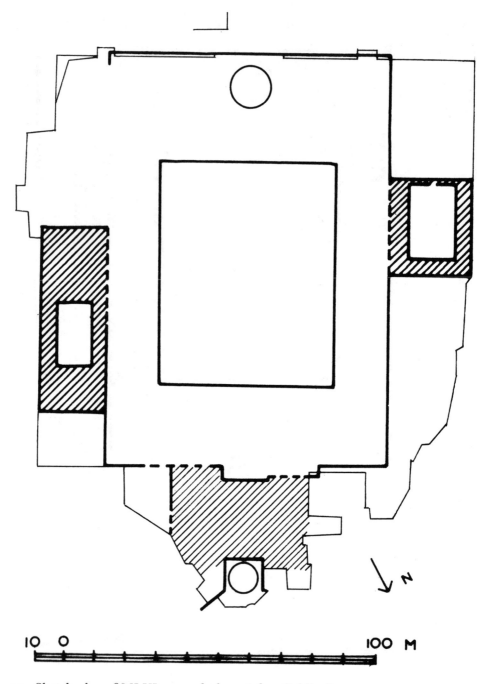

10 0   100 M

51. Sketch plan of MJ VI, second phase (after Galdieri).

136

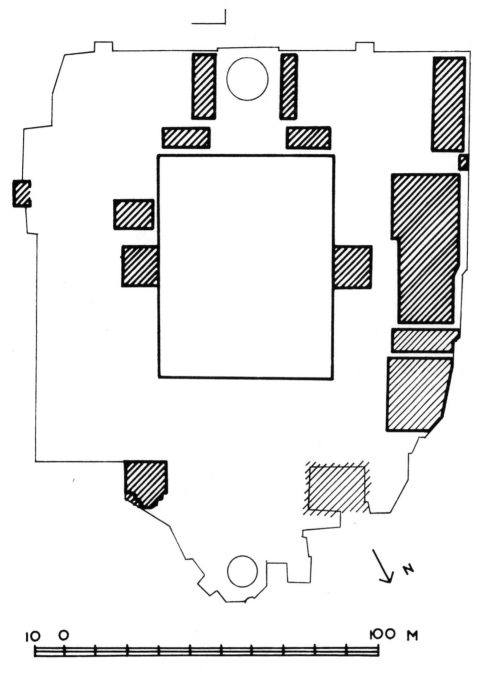

52. Safavid mosque (after Galdieri).

Index

140